P9-DBV-793

*Florida State Fair*
# C·O·O·K·B·O·O·K
## First Edition

# Florida State Fair
# C·O·O·K·B·O·O·K

## First Edition


**Emma Taylor, Editor**

**State Fair Books**
**Indianapolis, Indiana**
**1991**

Photo Credits:

Front-cover photo—Jars courtesy of the Ball Corporation, Muncie, Indiana
Back-cover photo—Courtesy of the Florida State Fair Authority, Tampa, Florida

Copyright ©1991 by the Florida State Fair Authority, Tampa, Florida

ISBN 0-89730-227-3

All rights reserved. No part of this publication may be reproduced, stored in a
retrieval system, or transmitted, in any form or by any means, electronic, mechanical,
photocopying, recording, or otherwise, without the prior written permission of the
copyright owner.

All inquiries should be addressed to:
FLORIDA STATE FAIR COOKBOOK
c/o State Fair Books
P. O. Box 90314
Indianapolis, IN 46290-0314

PRINTED IN THE UNITED STATES OF AMERICA

# CONTENTS

# PREFACE

The Florida State Fair kicked off the decade of the nineties by "Showcasing Florida" and by giving fairgoers the opportunity to experience the spirit of the Sunshine State. With that theme—"Showcase Florida"—in mind, we set out to compile recipes from some of Florida's best cooks for the first edition of the FLORIDA STATE FAIR COOKBOOK.

We gathered the contents of our book in much the same way a cook might assemble the ingredients for a special dish. We started by contacting blue-ribbon winners at the 1990 Florida State Fair, who provided us with recipes for their delectable baked goods and preserved foods. To these we added recipes from Sweepstakes award winners in the Youth and Young American divisions. (All of these prizewinning recipes are identified by "ribbons" next to the recipe names.)

We then turned to home economists at county extension units across the state and to commodity groups representing producers of Florida's bountiful fruits and vegetables as well as its fishes, game, beef, pork, and poultry. The Florida Department of Agriculture and Consumer Services, the Florida Game and Fresh Water Fish Commission, and the Florida Department of Citrus—along with numerous other organizations—contributed a variety of recipes featuring delicious new twists to old favorites.

For the finishing touch, we obtained recipes from some of Florida's master home chefs and from friends of the Florida State Fair. These recipes have stood the test of time and they continue to be family favorites on tables across the state of Florida.

This collection of more than 200 recipes is an attempt to convey the tastes and flavors of Florida's best baking, cooking, and home canning. From elegant appetizers and entrees to down-home stews and desserts, the FLORIDA STATE FAIR COOKBOOK, FIRST EDITION, truly offers something for everyone.

As an added bonus, all of the Florida State Fair Authority's royalties from the sale of this cookbook will be donated to the Family Living Center on the Florida State Fairgrounds.

So, in the spirit of the Sunshine State, we invite you to sample some of our favorite recipes—and enjoy!

—*Emma Taylor*
*Assistant Director*
*Florida State Fair Authority*

# Florida State Fair
## C·O·O·K·B·O·O·K
### First Edition

# APPETIZERS

Cucumber Dip   **12**
Robin's Grapefruit Dip   **12**
Tomato and Bacon Dip   **12**
Creamy Speckled Perch Dip   **13**
Smoked Fish Spread   **13**
Spicy Seven-Layer Dip   **14**
Catfish Balls   **14**
Tangy Meatballs   **15**

# Cucumber Dip

1 large or 2 small cucumbers, sliced
1 medium onion, sliced
¼ cup vinegar
1 teaspoon salt
Water
1 (8-ounce) package cream cheese,
    softened
¼ cup mayonnaise
1 teaspoon lime juice
1 tablespoon chopped chives
Green food coloring (optional)

Place cucumbers and onion in bowl; add vinegar, salt, and enough water to cover vegetables. Marinate for 30 minutes, then drain off liquid. Grind or chop vegetables; drain again by placing vegetables in cheesecloth and squeezing out moisture. Combine vegetables with cream cheese; add mayonnaise, lime juice, and chives, mixing thoroughly. A few drops of green food coloring may be added, if desired. Serve with fresh raw vegetables or chips.

*Florida Department of Agriculture and Consumer Services*

# Robin's Grapefruit Dip

1 cup dairy sour cream
1 tablespoon honey
Juice of 1 grapefruit

In small bowl, combine all ingredients; mix together until smooth and creamy. Serve with potato chips, crackers, and fresh raw vegetables.

Makes 1 cup dip.

*Florida Department of Citrus*

# Tomato and Bacon Dip

6 slices bacon
1 medium tomato
1 (8-ounce) package cream cheese,
    softened
2 teaspoons prepared mustard
½ teaspoon celery salt
¼ cup finely chopped green pepper
Assorted vegetables to use as "dippers"

Fry bacon until crisp; drain and crumble, then set aside. Peel and seed tomato; chop fine, then set aside. In small bowl, stir together cream cheese, mustard, and celery salt. Add bacon, tomato, and green pepper; mix well. Cover and chill. Serve with raw vegetable "dippers."

Makes 2 cups dip.

*Florida Department of Agriculture and Consumer Services*

# Creamy Speckled Perch Dip

2 pounds pan-dressed speckled perch or other small fish (fresh or frozen)
3 cups water
1 tablespoon salt
½ pint (1 cup) small-curd cottage cheese
½ pint (1 cup) dairy sour cream or plain yogurt
½ cup shredded raw carrot
¼ cup chopped sweet pickle, well drained
2 tablespoons chopped pimiento
1 tablespoon horseradish
2 teaspoons salt
Chopped parsley (for garnish)
Assorted chips, crackers, or crisp raw vegetables

Thaw fish if frozen. In large pan, combine water and one tablespoon salt; bring to boil. Place fish in boiling water. Cover pan, reduce heat, and simmer for 8-10 minutes or until fish flakes easily when tested with a fork. Drain fish; cool slightly. Remove and discard skin and bones; flake fish and chill. Combine cottage cheese, sour cream, carrot, pickle, pimiento, horseradish, and two teaspoons salt; mix well. Add flaked fish; stir well. Chill several hours. Sprinkle with parsley and serve with chips, crackers, or crisp raw vegetables.

Makes about 1 quart dip.

*Florida Game and Fresh Water Fish Commission*

# Smoked Fish Spread

1½ pounds smoked fish (preferably smoked mullet)
2 teaspoons minced onion
2 teaspoons minced celery
1 clove garlic, minced
2 tablespoons minced sweet pickle
1½ cups mayonnaise
1 tablespoon mustard
2 tablespoons chopped fresh parsley
1 teaspoon celery seed
Dash of Worcestershire sauce

Remove and discard skin and bones from fish; flake fish meat with a fork. Combine flaked fish with all remaining ingredients; mix well. Chill for at least 1 hour (overnight is better). Serve with crackers.

Makes 3½ cups spread.

*Doris Beauchamp, Cedar Key*

# Spicy Seven-Layer Dip

3 ripe avocados
2 tablespoons lemon juice
Salt and pepper to taste
1 package taco seasoning
1 cup dairy sour cream
½ cup mayonnaise
2 cans bean dip or 1 can refried beans
1 cup chopped green onions
3 medium tomatoes, chopped
1 (6-ounce) can pitted black olives, chopped
8 ounces shredded sharp cheddar cheese

In small bowl, mash avocados. Add lemon juice, salt, and pepper; mix well. In another bowl, combine taco seasoning, sour cream, and mayonnaise; mix well. Layer ingredients on a large round tray (or two small trays) in the following order: Spread bean dip on tray, then spread with avocado mixture, followed by seasoned sour cream, onions, tomatoes, olives, and cheese. Serve with chips for dipping. Enjoy!

NOTE: You can use two cans of guacamole dip in place of the avocados, lemon juice, salt, and pepper.

*Sandy Payant, Tampa*

# Catfish Balls

½ cup chopped bell pepper
½ cup chopped onion
Water
2 cups flaked cooked catfish
2 eggs, beaten
½ teaspoon red pepper
½ teaspoon salt
1 cup crushed saltines
1 tablespoon prepared mustard
Dash of Tabasco sauce
1 to 2 tablespoons flour (optional)
Oil for deep-frying
Prepared mustard

In saucepan, combine bell pepper and onion with small amount of water; boil until vegetables are tender. Drain vegetables, then mix with all remaining ingredients. If needed, add flour to thicken mixture. Drop by spoonfuls into hot oil; fry until golden brown, about 2-3 minutes. Serve with prepared mustard for dipping.

*Nell Deal, Westville*
*Farm-Raised Catfish Cookoff Finalist*

# Tangy Meatballs

*1½ pounds hot bulk sausage*
*½ pound ground beef*
*½ cup soft bread crumbs*
*1 egg*
*¼ cup chopped onion*
*1 teaspoon garlic salt*
*1 (12-ounce) jar chili sauce*
*1 cup catsup*
*1 teaspoon grated lime peel*
*2 tablespoons lime juice*
*1 tablespoon Worcestershire sauce*
*¼ to ½ teaspoon red pepper*
*½ teaspoon garlic salt*

In large bowl, combine sausage, ground beef, bread crumbs, egg, onion, and one teaspoon garlic salt; mix thoroughly. Form mixture into one-inch balls. Place meatballs on baking sheet; bake at 350°F for 20 minutes.

In large skillet, combine chili sauce, catsup, lime peel, lime juice, Worcestershire sauce, red pepper, and ½ teaspoon garlic salt. Add cooked meatballs to mixture in skillet; simmer for 20 minutes. Serve meatballs in chafing dish with sauce.

Makes 40-50 meatballs.

*Florida Department of Agriculture and Consumer Services*

# SALADS

Avocado and Ham Salad  **18**
Black Bing Salad  **18**
Crabmeat Mold  **19**
Emerald Coast Crunch Salad  **19**
Gold Coast Salad  **20**
Greek Salad  **20**
Pasta Salad Neptune  **21**
Seafood Salad  **21**
Skillet Slaw  **22**
Snowtop Cranberry Salad  **22**
Spinach Star Salad  **23**
Watermelon Salad with Celery-Nut Dressing  **23**
Broccoli Salad  **24**
Wonderful Blue Cheese Dressing  **24**

# Avocado and Ham Salad

1 ripe avocado, peeled and cubed
2 apples, cubed
3 tablespoons lime juice
2 cups cubed cooked ham
½ cup chopped celery
1 tablespoon minced green onion
Lettuce leaves
⅓ cup chopped pecans
Avocado and apple slices (for garnish, if desired)

**DRESSING**

¼ cup light cream
½ cup mayonnaise
¼ cup crumbled blue cheese

In large bowl, combine avocado, apples, and lime juice; toss to coat. Add ham, celery, and green onion; mix lightly. Pour dressing over salad mixture; toss to coat. Chill. Serve salad on individual lettuce-lined plates; sprinkle chopped pecans over each salad. Garnish with slices of avocado and apple, if desired.

To make Dressing: In blender container, combine cream, mayonnaise, and blue cheese; process until almost smooth.

Serves 6-8.

*Florida Department of Agriculture and Consumer Services*

# Black Bing Salad

2 cans black Bing cherries (reserve 1 cup juice)
1 package cherry Jello
1 cup Port wine
1 tablespoon unflavored gelatin
½ cup sugar
1 cup chopped nuts
2 teaspoons (approximately) lemon juice

Drain cherries, reserving one cup juice. Prepare Jello according to package directions, using cherry juice and Port wine as liquid. Stir cherries, gelatin, sugar, and nuts into Jello. Add lemon juice to taste (should be tart). Chill overnight or until firm.

Serves 8.

NOTE: Serve with a dollop of mayonnaise on top. Good with a dinner of game.

*Joyce Covington, Brandon*

# Crabmeat Mold

2 envelopes unflavored gelatin
1 cup water
1 (10-ounce) can condensed cream of
   shrimp soup
3 (3-ounce) packages cream cheese
6 green onions, finely chopped
2½ cups crabmeat
1 cup mayonnaise
1½ teaspoons lemon juice
2 teaspoons red-pepper sauce
1 teaspoon seasoned salt

In small bowl, combine gelatin and water; let stand to soften gelatin. In saucepan, combine soup and cream cheese; heat until warm and cream cheese is melted. Add softened gelatin to mixture in saucepan, then stir in all remaining ingredients. Pour mixture into oiled one-quart fish or shell mold. Cool for 10 minutes, then refrigerate for 8 hours. Serve with crackers or on lettuce leaves.

Serves 16.

NOTE: Beautiful when removed from mold and placed on a large serving platter—and delicious!

*Mrs. William O. Higgins, Tampa*

# Emerald Coast Crunch Salad

6 to 8 slices bacon
3 ounces sliced almonds
4 teaspoons sesame seeds
4 green onions, chopped
1 head lettuce, broken into pieces
½ cup Chinese noodles

**DRESSING**

4 tablespoons sugar
2 teaspoons salt
2 teaspoons Ac'cent
¼ teaspoon pepper
2 tablespoons vinegar
½ cup salad oil

In skillet, fry bacon until crisp. Drain and crumble bacon (reserve drippings); set bacon aside. Add almonds and sesame seeds to drippings in skillet; heat, stirring occasionally, until toasted. (Watch carefully or they will burn). In large bowl, combine bacon, almonds, and sesame seeds with all remaining salad ingredients. Pour dressing over salad; toss to mix before serving.

To make Dressing: Combine all ingredients; mix well.

Serves 6.

NOTE: This is a crisp, crunchy change from regular green salad.

*Lynda Ray, Baker*

# Gold Coast Salad

Lettuce leaves
1 pound shrimp, cooked, peeled and
   deveined
2 oranges, peeled and sliced
1 grapefruit, peeled and sliced
2 medium tomatoes, cut into wedges
1 red bell pepper, seeded and sliced
1 avocado, peeled and cut into wedges
½ cup sliced celery
½ cup pitted black olives

## GOLD COAST SALAD DRESSING

1 cup dairy sour cream
2 tablespoons frozen concentrated
   orange juice, thawed (undiluted)
1 tablespoon Dijon-style mustard
2 teaspoons prepared horseradish
2 green onions, finely chopped

Place lettuce leaves on large serving
plate. Arrange all remaining
ingredients on lettuce. Serve with Gold
Coast Salad Dressing.

To make Gold Coast Salad Dressing: In
small bowl, combine sour cream,
orange juice concentrate, mustard, and
horseradish; fold in chopped green
onions. Cover, then chill for about 1
hour. (Makes 1¼ cups dressing.)

Serves 4.

Florida Department of Citrus

# Greek Salad

1 large head lettuce
12 roka leaves or watercress sprigs
2 tomatoes, each cut into six wedges
1 cucumber, peeled and cut lengthwise
   into eight "fingers"
1 avocado, peeled and cut into wedges
4 portions feta cheese
4 slices canned beets
4 anchovy fillets
12 medium-hot Salonika peppers
   (available in bottles)
4 fancy-cut radishes
1 bell pepper, cut into eight rings
3 cups potato salad
4 shrimp, cooked and peeled
12 black Greek olives
4 whole green onions
½ cup distilled white vinegar
¼ cup olive oil
¼ cup salad oil
Oregano (to taste)

Arrange all prepared salad ingredients
on a large platter in the order listed.
Sprinkle vinegar over entire salad.
Combine olive oil with salad oil;
drizzle over salad. Sprinkle oregano
over top of salad before serving.

Serves 4.

Pinellas County Cooperative Extension
Service, Largo

# Pasta Salad Neptune

½ pound fusilli (pasta), broken into
    two-inch pieces
2 tablespoons olive oil
1 tablespoon white wine vinegar
⅓ cup grapefruit juice, divided
1 pound frozen imitation crabmeat,
    thawed and cut into one-inch pieces
3 cups broccoli florets, steamed until
    tender-crisp
2 cups fresh spinach leaves, torn into
    coarse pieces
1 cup cherry tomatoes, halved
2 green onions, sliced
2 grapefruit, peeled and sectioned

**DRESSING**

Grapefruit juice (see above)
⅔ cup mayonnaise
¼ cup coarsely chopped fresh basil
    leaves or 1 tablespoon dried leaf
    basil
½ cup fresh parsley leaves
2 tablespoons Dijon-style mustard

Cook pasta according to package directions; drain. In large bowl, combine pasta with oil, vinegar, and one tablespoon grapefruit juice; mix well. Gently fold in imitation crabmeat, broccoli, spinach, tomatoes, onions, and grapefruit sections. Pour dressing over pasta mixture. Toss lightly to coat well.

To make Dressing: In food processor or blender container, combine remaining grapefruit juice (about ¼ cup), mayonnaise, basil, parsley, and mustard; process until smooth.

Serves 6.

*Florida Department of Citrus*

# Seafood Salad

6 to 8 ounces crabmeat or imitation
    crabmeat, cooked
8 to 10 ounces shrimp (fresh or frozen),
    cooked
1 (8-ounce) can water chestnuts, sliced
4 to 5 ounces fresh mushrooms, sliced
2 cups sliced celery
2 very small scallions, sliced
1 (2½-ounce) package sliced almonds
4 eggs, hard-cooked and sliced
1 teaspoon salt
1 pint Hellman's mayonnaise

Combine all ingredients in order listed; toss gently. Refrigerate overnight or at least 2-3 hours before serving.

Serves 8-10 for luncheon.

*Martha Woeste, Gainesville*

# Skillet Slaw

1 slice bacon
1 tablespoon finely chopped onion
1 tablespoon vinegar
1 tablespoon water
¾ teaspoon sugar
Pinch of salt
Pepper to taste
1 cup shredded cabbage
½ small apple, pared and chopped fine
3 tablespoons dairy sour cream

In small skillet, fry bacon until crisp. Drain and crumble bacon (reserve drippings); set bacon aside. Add onion to bacon drippings in skillet; cook for 2 minutes. Stir in vinegar, water, sugar, salt, and pepper; bring just to a boil. Add cabbage and apple; toss to coat. Cover and cook over medium heat for 5 minutes or just until cabbage wilts. Stir in sour cream; top with crumbled bacon.

Serves 2.

*Florida Department of Agriculture and Consumer Services*

# Snowtop Cranberry Salad

1 (6-ounce) package raspberry-flavored gelatin
1 teaspoon plain gelatin
2 cups boiling water
1½ cups chopped pecans, divided
1 cup cranapple juice
1 (8-ounce) can crushed pineapple (undrained)
1 cup diced celery
1 (16-ounce) can whole cranberry sauce
1 (3-ounce) package cream cheese, softened
1 cup dairy sour cream
Lettuce leaves

In mixing bowl, combine raspberry gelatin, plain gelatin, and boiling water. Stir mixture until gelatin is dissolved, then cool. Add one cup pecans, cranapple juice, pineapple, celery, and cranberry sauce; mix well. Pour mixture into oiled two-quart casserole; refrigerate until firm. In small bowl, beat cream cheese until fluffy; gradually add sour cream, mixing well. Spread creamed mixture over firm gelatin; sprinkle with remaining ½ cup pecans. Refrigerate for several hours. Cut into squares and serve on lettuce leaves.

Serves 12.

*Florida Department of Agriculture and Consumer Services*

# Spinach Star Salad

4 ounces fresh spinach, washed and
trimmed
4 ounces cooked turkey or chicken
breast, cut into julienne strips
1 cup ripe avocado cubes, sprinkled
with lime juice
1 large tomato, cut into eight wedges
1 small white onion, sliced and
separated into rings
1 carambola*, cut into star-slices
Oil and vinegar dressing

In large serving bowl, combine spinach, turkey or chicken strips, avocado cubes, tomato wedges, onion rings, and carambola star-slices; toss lightly. Serve with oil and vinegar dressing.

Serves 4.

*NOTE: Often called "star fruit," the carambola earned its name from its star-shaped slices when cut into cross-sections. Select firm, shiny-skinned fruit and allow to ripen at room temperature.

*Nan Brooks, Homestead*

# Watermelon Salad with Celery-Nut Dressing

3 to 4 cups watermelon balls, chilled
Lettuce leaves (optional)
½ cup chopped pecans

**CELERY-NUT DRESSING**

4 ounces cream cheese, softened
2 tablespoons mayonnaise
⅓ cup whipping cream
1⅓ cups finely diced celery

Spoon watermelon balls into sherbet or champagne glasses, or arrange melon balls on lettuce leaves on individual serving plates, if desired. Spoon dressing over melon balls. Sprinkle pecans over top.

To make Celery-Nut Dressing: In mixing bowl, beat cream cheese until light and fluffy. Add mayonnaise; beat until smooth and well blended. In another bowl, beat whipping cream until soft peaks form. Fold whipped cream into cream-cheese mixture, then fold in celery.

Serves 6.

NOTE: Watermelon balls become an elegant first-course salad when served in a compote with creamy celery-nut dressing as a topping.

*Sandy Russell, Gainesville*

# Broccoli Salad

2 bunches broccoli, separated into
  small florets
1 medium red onion, diced
½ cup white raisins
10 to 12 slices bacon, fried and
  crumbled
1 cup mayonnaise (I use light
  mayonnaise)
2 tablespoons vinegar
2 teaspoons sugar

In large bowl, combine broccoli, onion, raisins, and bacon. In another bowl, combine mayonnaise, vinegar, and sugar; mix well. Pour dressing over salad; marinate for 1-2 hours before serving.

*Edna Wainwright, Starke*

# Wonderful Blue Cheese Dressing
## (Made with Food Processor)

1 (8-ounce) package cream cheese, cut
  into one-inch pieces
½ cup mayonnaise
½ teaspoon garlic salt
½ cup milk
4 ounces blue cheese, cut into one-inch
  cubes

Combine cream cheese, mayonnaise, and garlic salt in food processor container; pulse until smooth, about 3-5 seconds. With processor running, pour milk through food chute slowly. Add blue cheese to container and pulse to mix, about 5 seconds.

Makes 2 cups salad dressing.

NOTE: To reduce fat content, use light cream cheese, light mayonnaise, and skim milk.

*Sandy Blackadar, Lithia*

# SOUPS, CHILIES & STEWS

## Fast-Track Clam Chowder

2 slices bacon
¼ cup chopped onion
1 tablespoon flour
Salt and pepper to taste
1 can Gordon's minced clams (drain
    and reserve liquid)
1 bottle clam broth
2 medium potatoes, peeled and cubed
1 cup half-and-half
Few drops of Tabasco sauce
Parsley (for garnish)

In microwave, cook bacon until crisp; crumble and set aside, reserving one tablespoon drippings. In skillet, sauté onion in bacon drippings; stir in flour, salt, and pepper. Add liquid from clams, bottled clam broth, and potatoes; bring to boil, stirring constantly. Reduce heat until mixture is simmering; cook uncovered until potatoes are tender. Add crumbled bacon, clams, half-and-half, and Tabasco sauce to taste; heat just until hot. Top with parsley.

Serves 3-4.

*Sylvia Schmidtetter, Anna Maria*

## Florida Grouper Chowder

2 fillets fresh grouper
1 large onion, finely chopped
2 tablespoons butter
2 sprigs fresh parsley, minced, or 1½
    teaspoons dried parsley
2 large potatoes, peeled and diced
2 tablespoons water
1 (No. 2) can tomatoes
Salt and pepper to taste
Celery seed

Cut grouper fillets into small pieces; remove and discard any bones, then set fish aside. In skillet, sauté onion in butter. Add parsley, potatoes, and water; cover and steam until potatoes are cooked. Add tomatoes; bring mixture to a boil. Add fish to mixture in skillet; cook for 10 minutes. Season to taste. Sprinkle with celery seed before serving.

Serves 4.

NOTE: This recipe can be made with other flaky fish, but not with mullet.

*C. P. Packett, Tallahassee*

# Shirley's Chili with a Snap

2½ pounds coarsely ground chuck
½ pound pork sausage
1½ teaspoons crushed garlic
1½ cups chopped white onion
1 green pepper, chopped
1 tablespoon beef base or bouillon
1 tablespoon dried basil
1 teaspoon dried oregano
1 tablespoon ground cumin seed
1 tablespoon chili powder
¾ teaspoon freshly ground black pepper
½ cup dried parsley
1½ teaspoons dried dill
1 lemon, thinly sliced
1 (12-ounce) can tomato paste
2 tablespoons Dijon-style mustard
¼ cup hearty Burgundy wine
3 (1-pound) cans plum tomatoes,
    drained and crushed with hands
2 cans kidney beans, drained (optional)

In large skillet, brown ground chuck and sausage with garlic, onion, and green pepper; do not drain off drippings. Add beef base or bouillon, herbs, and spices; heat thoroughly. Add lemon slices, tomato paste, mustard, wine, and tomatoes; mix well. Simmer chili on low heat for 2 hours, stirring occasionally. Add kidney beans, if desired. Serve chili with bowls of grated cheddar cheese, sour cream, chopped green onion, and nacho chips.

Serves 8-10.

NOTE: This recipe won first prize in the Florida Cowbelles Chili Cookoff at the 1982 Florida State Fair.

*Shirley J. Myrsiades, Clearwater*

# Weird Chili

1½ pounds ground chuck
1½ pounds lean pork sausage
2 cups chopped onions
6 cloves garlic, minced
2 tablespoons sugar
1 tablespoon unsweetened cocoa
    powder
¼ cup chili powder (or to taste—you
    be the judge)
2 (15-ounce) cans tomato sauce
2 (15-ounce) cans tomatoes, crushed
2 (15-ounce) cans kidney beans
1 small can tomato paste
1 (12-ounce) can beer
Pepper, cumin, and paprika to taste

In large skillet, combine ground chuck, sausage, and onions. Cook until done, then drain and return to skillet. Add all remaining ingredients; mix well. Cover and simmer for at least 2 hours.

*Carlota Robinson, Tampa*
*Robinson's Racing Pigs*

## Vegetable and Beef Chili

1 large onion, finely chopped
2 large garlic cloves, minced
1 tablespoon olive oil
1 pound ground round
1 (28-ounce) can tomatoes in puree
2 tablespoons brown sugar
2 tablespoons chili powder
1 tablespoon cumin
1 tablespoon oregano
½ teaspoon salt
½ teaspoon black pepper
2 cups cooked kidney beans
1 cup sliced carrots
1 cup diced celery
1 cup diced green pepper
1 cup corn (fresh or frozen)

In skillet, sauté onion and garlic in olive oil until tender. Add ground round; brown with onion and garlic, then drain off fat. Add tomatoes, brown sugar, chili powder, cumin, oregano, salt, and black pepper; mix well. Heat until bubbling, then reduce heat; cover and simmer for 45 minutes. Add kidney beans, carrots, celery, and green pepper; mix well. Cover and continue to simmer for about 45 minutes. Add corn; continue to simmer for an additional 20 minutes or until mixture reaches desired thickness. Taste and adjust seasonings as desired.

Serves 6-8.

NOTE: When served over brown rice, this is a delicious cold-weather meal. For vegetarians, the meat can be omitted and the dish will still be complete when served with rice.

*Marcia Zabor, Ocala*
*Marion County Extension Home Economist*

## Vegetarian Chili

3 bell peppers (one green, one red, one
   yellow), chopped
1 medium onion, chopped
1 tablespoon olive oil
1 package chili seasoning mix
1 (8-ounce) can tomato sauce
1 can red kidney beans
1 can black beans
1 can garbanzo beans, drained
1 can hominy, drained
Shredded cheese (for garnish)

In large kettle, brown peppers and onion in olive oil. Add chili seasoning and tomato sauce; simmer and stir, cooking according to directions on seasoning package. Add all beans and hominy; mix well. Simmer for 45 minutes. Garnish with shredded cheese before serving.

Serves 6-8.

NOTE: You may add more of one kind of bean than another, depending on your preference.

*Rosanne Miller, Lutz*

# Fresh Florida Vegetable Stew

1 cup chopped fresh onions
1 tablespoon butter
5 extra-large tomatoes, cut into small
    pieces (one inch or less)
1½ teaspoons salt
¼ teaspoon sugar
¼ teaspoon pepper
2 cups cubed potatoes (cut ½ inch
    thick)
1½ cups fresh green beans, cut into
    one-inch pieces
1 cup carrot slices (cut ½ inch thick)
2 medium ears of corn

In large saucepan, sauté onions in butter until tender. Add tomatoes, salt, sugar, and pepper; stir to mix. Cover and simmer for 20 minutes. Prepare potatoes, beans, and carrots; set aside. Remove husks and silks from ears of corn; rinse corn. Using a sharp knife, cut corn kernels from cobs; discard cobs and set corn aside. Add potatoes, beans, and carrots to mixture in skillet; stir. Cover and cook about 20 minutes. Add corn kernels; cover and cook an additional 10-15 minutes or until vegetables are tender.

Serves 8.

NOTE: Each serving provides 126 calories, 3 g protein, 26 g carbohydrates, and 2 g fat.

*Florida Department of Agriculture and Consumer Services*

# Fisherman's Bass Stew

½ cup chopped onion
2 tablespoons cooking oil
2 (10¾-ounce) cans cream of potato
    soup
2 cups milk
1 (1-pound) can tomato wedges,
    undrained
1 (10-ounce) package frozen mixed
    vegetables, thawed
1 (8-ounce) can whole-kernel corn,
    drained
1 teaspoon salt
⅛ teaspoon pepper
1 small bay leaf
1 pound bass fillets, cut into one-inch
    pieces

In large pot, cook onion in oil until tender but not brown. Add soup, milk, tomato wedges, mixed vegetables, corn, salt, pepper, and bay leaf; heat, stirring occasionally, until simmering. Add fish; simmer for approximately 10 minutes or until fish flakes easily when tested with a fork.

Serves 6.

*Florida Game and Fresh Water Fish Commission*

# Healthy, Hearty Italian Stew
## (Pasta e Fagioli)

1 teaspoon olive oil
6 cloves garlic
1 medium onion, chopped
1½ pounds ground turkey
2 (14½-ounce) cans Italian tomatoes, crushed
1½ cups water
1 can kidney beans, drained
1 can cannelloni beans, drained
½ teaspoon oregano
½ teaspoon basil
½ teaspoon fennel
¾ cup julienned carrots
¾ cup sliced celery and chopped celery tops
½ pound small pasta shells

Heat oil in Dutch oven. Crush two cloves of garlic. Sauté crushed garlic and onion in hot oil until brown. Add ground turkey and brown well, breaking into chunks with spatula. Add tomatoes, water, beans, and spices. Crush remaining garlic and add to mixture. Add carrots and celery. Bring to boil, then reduce heat and simmer for 20 minutes. Bring to boil again, then add pasta shells. Reduce heat and continue cooking for 10 minutes or until shells are "al dente." Serve hot with crusty bread.

Serves 6.

NOTE: We have trimmed the fat from this old Italian favorite. Just one taste and you'll be hooked!

*Paula and David Citron, Tamarac
Broward County Fair*

# Alligator Stew

½ cup cooking oil
1 quart alligator meat, cut into small pieces about ½ inch thick
½ cup chopped green onions
½ cup chopped onions
½ cup chopped bell pepper
½ cup chopped celery
1 (10-ounce) can Rotel tomatoes (do not drain)
2 tablespoons minced parsley
Salt and pepper to taste
Hot cooked rice

In large pot, heat cooking oil; add meat and brown on all sides. Add chopped vegetables, Rotel tomatoes, and seasonings. Cover pot and cook over medium heat for 30-40 minutes. Serve over hot cooked rice.

*Mrs. Charles Herbert*

# MAIN DISHES

## Chicken

Lime Barbecued Chicken   33
South-of-the-Border Chicken Bake   33
Plantation Chicken   34
Baked Chicken and Orzo   34
Cantonese Chicken   35
Chicken with Peppers and Walnuts   36

## Fish & Shellfish

All-American Fried Fish   37
Jiffy Broiled Speckled Perch   37
Viva Tilapia   38
Catfish Calhoun   38
Gourmet Bream   39
Shrimp Jambalaya   39
Vegetable-Stuffed Catfish   40
Herbed Clam Fritters   40
Fried Eel with Tartar Sauce   41

(Continued)

# Meats

# One-Dish Meals

# Chicken

## Lime Barbecued Chicken

¼ cup Mazola corn oil
1 broiler-fryer chicken, cut into serving
  pieces
1 teaspoon Ac'cent
1 teaspoon salt

**LIME SAUCE**

1 clove garlic
½ teaspoon salt
½ cup lime juice
2 tablespoons grated onion
½ teaspoon thyme
¼ teaspoon black pepper

Heat corn oil in frying pan over medium heat. Sprinkle chicken with Ac'cent and salt. Place chicken in frying pan and brown on all sides. Pour Lime Sauce over chicken in skillet. Reduce heat, cover, and cook for about 40 minutes or until fork can be inserted in chicken with ease. Baste frequently during cooking.

To make Lime Sauce: In small bowl, crush garlic with salt. Add lime juice, onion, thyme, and pepper; mix thoroughly.

Serves 4.

*Lucille B. Bateman, Orlando*
*Florida Chicken Cooking Contest Finalist*

## South-of-the-Border Chicken Bake

½ cup creamed cottage cheese or Ricotta
  cheese
1 (3-ounce) package cream cheese,
  softened
1 cup dairy sour cream
⅛ teaspoon garlic powder
1 (4-ounce) can chilies, chopped
3 cups chopped cooked chicken (cut in
  large pieces)
3 cups cooked rice (cook rice in chicken
  broth)
1½ cups (6 ounces) shredded cheese
½ cup pitted ripe olives
1 cup crushed corn chips
½ cup shredded cheese

In large mixing bowl, combine cottage cheese, cream cheese, and sour cream; blend well. Add garlic powder and chilies. Fold in chicken and rice. Add 1½ cups shredded cheese and olives; mix thoroughly. Pour mixture into greased three-quart baking dish. Mix crushed corn chips with ½ cup shredded cheese; sprinkle over top of mixture in baking dish. Bake at 350°F for 25-30 minutes.

Serves 10 or more.

NOTE: This is a nice luncheon dish that I have used many times. Serve with a fresh fruit salad and tea.

*Barbara Sapp, Williston*

# Plantation Chicken

1 cup diced celery
Boiling water
1 medium onion, chopped
2 tablespoons minced green pepper
5 tablespoons margarine
6 tablespoons flour
3 cups milk
1 (10-ounce) can cream of mushroom
   soup
4 cups diced cooked chicken
2 tablespoons canned pimiento
Salt to taste
1 cup soft bread crumbs
1 cup grated cheese

Cook celery in one inch of boiling water until tender, then drain and set aside. In skillet, sauté onion and green pepper in margarine; add flour and blend together. Add milk and cook over low heat, stirring constantly, until mixture is smooth. Add soup, chicken, pimiento, and celery; heat well. Add salt to taste. Pour mixture into greased two-quart casserole dish. Combine bread crumbs with cheese; sprinkle over top of mixture in casserole. Bake in moderately hot oven (375°F) for 30 minutes or until golden brown. May be served in pastry shells, if desired.

Serves 12.

*Carolyn Chasteen, Lake City*

# Baked Chicken and Orzo

1 (3½- to 4-pound) roasting chicken, cut
   up
1 teaspoon crushed garlic
1 tablespoon tomato paste
¼ teaspoon freshly ground black pepper
Salt to taste
½ cup (1 stick) butter or margarine
2½ cups chicken broth
1 bay leaf
1 cup orzo macaroni (uncooked)

Rinse chicken pieces; pat dry with paper towels. (If desired, you may remove the skin from the chicken.) Rub chicken pieces with garlic, then place in oiled 13x9x2½-inch casserole dish. Coat chicken pieces with tomato paste; sprinkle with pepper and salt, and dot with butter or margarine. Bake at 350°F for 30 minutes.

In saucepan, bring broth to boil. Take casserole from oven; remove chicken from casserole dish and set aside, keeping warm. Add hot broth, bay leaf, and orzo to casserole dish; mix well. Arrange chicken pieces on top of orzo. Cover casserole with foil and bake for 30-40 minutes or until orzo is cooked. Remove casserole dish from oven; replace foil with a few paper towels to absorb any extra moisture. Let casserole sit for 15 minutes before serving.

*Shirley J. Myrsiades, Clearwater*

# Cantonese Chicken

½ cup soy sauce
1 tablespoon meat seasoning
1 teaspoon Ac'cent
½ teaspoon ground ginger
½ teaspoon sugar
½ teaspoon freshly ground black pepper
1 broiler-fryer chicken, cut in pieces
½ cup Mazola corn oil
1 (8-ounce) can water chestnuts, drained and sliced
1 (8½-ounce) can bamboo shoots, drained
1 (4-ounce) can sliced mushrooms, drained (reserve liquid)
1/3 cup sliced celery
1 tablespoon cornstarch
2 tablespoons cold water
1 cup broth (made from mushroom liquid, chicken-flavored bouillon cube and boiling water)
2 green onions, sliced
Hot cooked rice

In deep bowl, mix together soy sauce, meat seasoning, Ac'cent, ginger, sugar, and pepper. Add chicken pieces, turning to coat. Marinate in refrigerator for 2 hours, turning chicken pieces two or three times. Remove chicken; reserve marinade. Heat corn oil in frying pan over medium heat. Add chicken and brown on all sides. Cover and cook on low heat for 30 minutes or until fork can be inserted in chicken with ease. Remove chicken from skillet; drain off all but ¼ cup drippings. Add water chestnuts, bamboo shoots, mushrooms, and celery to skillet; cook, stirring frequently, for about 5 minutes. Combine cornstarch and water, then stir into vegetables. Stir in broth and reserved marinade. Cook and stir until mixture is clear and smooth. Add chicken; heat thoroughly. Scatter green onions over top. Serve over hot rice.

Serves 4.

*Mary Ellen Fowler, Dania*
*Florida Chicken Cooking Contest Finalist*

# Chicken with Peppers and Walnuts

1½ *pounds boned and skinned chicken*
   *breasts*
3 *tablespoons soy sauce*
2 *teaspoons cornstarch*
2 *tablespoons dry sherry*
½ *teaspoon salt*
¼ *teaspoon ground ginger*
¼ *teaspoon crushed red pepper*
1 *teaspoon sugar*
2 *tablespoons peanut oil*
1 *cup walnut halves*
1 *clove garlic, finely minced*
2 *medium green peppers, cut into strips*
5 *green onions (including tops), sliced*
   *diagonally into one-inch pieces*
*Hot cooked rice*

Cut chicken into one-inch pieces; set aside. In small bowl, blend soy sauce with cornstarch. Stir in sherry, salt, ginger, red pepper, and sugar; set aside. Preheat wok or skillet to 375°F; add oil. Stir-fry walnuts for 1-2 minutes or just until golden; remove from wok and set aside. Add chicken and garlic to hot wok or skillet; stir-fry for 2-3 minutes. Push chicken up the sides of wok (or remove if using skillet); add peppers and onions and stir-fry for 2 minutes or until vegetables are tender-crisp. Stir soy-sauce mixture, then combine with chicken, peppers, and onions in wok or skillet. Heat, stirring constantly, until mixture has thickened and is bubbling; cover and cook for 1 additional minute. Add walnuts. Serve at once with hot cooked rice.

Serves 4-5.

*Florida Department of Agriculture and*
*Consumer Services*

# Fish & Shellfish

## All-American Fried Fish

*3 pounds pan-dressed (or 2 pounds
    fillets) blue gills, shellcrackers, or
    speckled perch*
*⅔ cup cornmeal or, for finer texture, 1/3
    cup cornmeal mixed with 1/3 cup all-
    purpose flour*
*2 teaspoons salt*
*½ teaspoon paprika*
*Cooking oil for frying*

Thaw fish if frozen. Clean fish thoroughly; pat dry with paper towels. Combine cornmeal, salt, and paprika. Roll fish in cornmeal mixture. In heavy frying pan, heat about ⅛ inch of oil until hot but not smoking. Fry fish in hot oil at moderate heat (360°F) for 4-5 minutes or until fish is brown. Carefully turn over fish; cook 4-5 minutes longer or until fish is brown on both sides and flakes easily when tested with a fork. Drain on absorbent paper.

Serves 6.

*Florida Game and Fresh Water Fish Commission*

## Jiffy Broiled Speckled Perch

*2 pounds speckled perch fillets (fresh or
    frozen)*
*2 tablespoons salad oil*
*2 tablespoons soy sauce*
*2 tablespoons Worcestershire sauce*
*1 teaspoon salt*
*1 teaspoon paprika*
*½ teaspoon chili powder*
*½ teaspoon garlic powder*
*Dash of liquid hot pepper sauce*
*Lemon wedges*

Thaw fish if frozen. Place fillets in a single layer, skin side down, on a well-greased 16x10-inch broil-and-serve platter. Combine all remaining ingredients except lemon wedges; pour sauce over fillets. Broil about four inches from source of heat for 8-10 minutes or until fish flakes easily when tested with a fork. Baste with sauce in pan once during broiling.

Serves 6.

*Florida Game and Fresh Water Fish Commission*

## Viva Tilapia

¼ *cup chopped celery*
¼ *cup chopped onion*
¼ *cup chopped sweet red pepper*
3 *tablespoons margarine or butter*
3 *tablespoons flour*
*Salt and pepper to taste*
½ *teaspoon dried tarragon*
½ *teaspoon dried basil*
1¼ *cups milk*
1 *cup shredded mozzarella cheese*
1½ *to 2 pounds tilapia fillets*

In medium skillet, sauté celery, onion, and red pepper in margarine until vegetables are tender. Add flour, salt, pepper, tarragon, and basil; mix well. Cook for 1 minute, stirring constantly. Gradually add milk and cook over medium heat, stirring constantly, until thickened. Add cheese; heat and stir until cheese is melted. Do not boil. Place fish fillets in 12x8x2-inch baking dish. Spoon sauce evenly over fish fillets. Bake at 425°F for 8-10 minutes or until fish flakes easily when tested with a fork.

Serves 4.

*Florida Game and Fresh Water Fish Commission*

## Catfish Calhoun

2 *pounds catfish fillets*
1 *cup light mayonnaise*
1 *cup dairy sour cream*
2 *tablespoons ranch-style bacon salad*
  *dressing mix*
¼ *cup finely chopped green onion*
3 *tablespoons lime juice or lemon juice*
1 *or 2 (2.8-ounce) cans french-fried*
  *onion rings, crushed*

Spray a two-quart baking dish with nonstick cooking spray; place fish fillets in dish. In mixing bowl, combine mayonnaise, sour cream, salad dressing mix, green onion, and lime or lemon juice; mix well. Spread mayonnaise mixture over fillets, completely covering fish. Top with crushed french-fried onion rings. Bake at 375°F for 20 minutes or until fish flakes easily when tested with a fork.

Serves 4.

NOTE: To cut down on fat and cholesterol, use light sour cream or yogurt, and top with croutons or bread crumbs instead of french-fried onion rings.

*Florida Game and Fresh Water Fish Commission*

# Gourmet Bream
## (Blue Gills)

3 pounds pan-dressed bream or other
   small fish (approximately 6 ounces
   each—fresh or frozen)
1 tablespoon salt
4 cups soft bread cubes (cut in ½-inch
   squares)
½ cup (1 stick) margarine, melted, or
   cooking oil
1 cup sliced fresh mushrooms
⅔ cup sliced green onions
½ teaspoon salt
¼ cup chopped fresh parsley
2 tablespoons chopped pimiento
4 teaspoons lemon juice
½ teaspoon marjoram
3 tablespoons margarine, melted, or
   cooking oil

Thaw fish if frozen. Clean fish thoroughly; pat dry with paper towels. Sprinkle one tablespoon salt evenly over inside and outside of fish. In skillet, sauté bread cubes in ½ cup margarine until lightly browned, stirring frequently. Add mushrooms and onions; cook until mushrooms are tender. Stir in remaining ½ teaspoon salt, parsley, pimiento, lemon juice, and marjoram; toss lightly. Stuff fish with bread-cube mixture. Arrange stuffed fish in a single layer in well-greased 13½x8¾x1¾-inch baking pan. Brush fish with remaining three tablespoons margarine. Bake in moderate oven (350°F) for 20-25 minutes or until fish flakes easily when tested with a fork. Serve plain or with your favorite fish sauce.

Serves 6.

*Florida Game and Fresh Water Fish Commission*

# Shrimp Jambalaya

3 tablespoons butter
½ teaspoon minced garlic
1 medium green pepper, chopped
1 small onion, sliced
8 ounces pork sausage
1 (28-ounce) can whole tomatoes
1 pound raw shrimp, cleaned
2 cups water
1 bay leaf
1 teaspoon salt
½ teaspoon black pepper
1 cup uncooked rice

In large saucepan, melt butter. Add garlic, green pepper, onion, and sausage; sauté for 5 minutes. Add tomatoes (breaking into pieces with a spoon), shrimp, water, and seasonings; bring to boil. Stir in rice. Reduce heat; cover and simmer until rice is fluffy, about 25 minutes. Remove bay leaf before serving.

Makes 6 one-cup servings.

*Sandy Blackadar, Lithia*

# Vegetable-Stuffed Catfish

6 pan-dressed catfish
2 teaspoons salt
6 slices bacon, cut in thirds
Paprika

**VEGETABLE STUFFING**

1 cup grated carrot
¾ cup chopped celery
½ cup chopped onion
⅓ cup butter
2 cups soft bread crumbs
1 tablespoon lime juice or lemon juice
½ teaspoon salt

To make Vegetable Stuffing: In saucepan, cook carrot, celery, and onion in butter until tender, stirring occasionally. Add bread crumbs, lime or lemon juice, and salt; mix lightly.

Sprinkle fish with salt. Stuff fish with Vegetable Stuffing. Place stuffed fish in well-greased 14x11x1-inch baking pan. Arrange three pieces of bacon on each fish. Sprinkle with paprika. Bake at 350°F for 25-30 minutes. When fish is done, turn on broiler; move fish three inches from source of heat and broil for 2-3 minutes or until bacon is crisp.

Serves 4.

*Florida Game and Fresh Water Fish Commission*

# Herbed Clam Fritters

2½ cups flour
1½ teaspoons salt
1½ teaspoons baking powder
¼ cup (½ stick) margarine or butter
3 eggs, separated
1 cup beer
2 dozen shucked clams (reserve liquor)
1 tablespoon parsley
⅛ teaspoon onion powder
⅛ scant teaspoon garlic powder
⅛ teaspoon pepper
Cooking oil for deep-frying

In large bowl, combine flour, salt, and baking powder. Melt margarine; stir into flour mixture. Lightly beat egg yolks; add to flour mixture and blend well. Gradually stir in beer, then set aside in warm place for 1 hour. Add clams, clam liquor, and seasonings. (If mixture is not of the proper consistency, add more flour or more beer.) Beat egg whites until stiff; fold into clam mixture. Heat oil to 375°F. Drop batter by tablespoonfuls into hot oil. Cook until fritters are golden brown, about 2-3 minutes.

Makes about 24 two-inch fritters.

*Florida Game and Fresh Water Fish Commission*

# Fried Eel

1 or 2 skinned and cleaned eels (about
   1¼ pounds total weight)
Milk
Salt and freshly ground pepper to taste
¼ teaspoon Tabasco sauce
½ cup flour
Oil for deep-frying
1 large bunch fresh parsley (optional)
Lemon wedges

## TARTAR SAUCE

1 egg yolk
1 teaspoon wine vinegar
2 tablespoons prepared mustard
   (preferably Dijon or Dusseldorf)
Few drops of Tabasco sauce
Salt and freshly ground black pepper to
   taste
1 cup olive oil (preferably a light olive
   oil or a combination of olive oil and
   peanut, vegetable or corn oil)
Lemon juice to taste (optional)
¼ cup finely chopped fresh parsley
3 tablespoons finely chopped green
   onion
¼ cup finely chopped cornichons or
   sour pickles
3 tablespoons chopped capers, drained

Cut eels into three-inch lengths. Place eel pieces in mixing bowl; add enough milk to cover along with salt, pepper, and Tabasco sauce. Let sit for 10 minutes. Drain well; dredge eel pieces in flour seasoned with salt and pepper. Heat oil in deep-fryer or skillet; when oil is hot and almost smoking, add eel pieces. Cook, stirring occasionally and turning the pieces, until golden brown and cooked through, about 5 minutes. Drain on paper toweling before serving.

Trim off and discard parsley stems. If parsley is totally clean, do not wash it; if rinsed, it must be patted completely dry. Add parsley to deep-fryer and fry until crisp, about 2 minutes. (Parsley will darken as it cooks.) Drain well and serve with eel pieces, lemon wedges, and tartar sauce.

To make Tartar Sauce: Place egg yolk in mixing bowl; add vinegar, mustard, Tabasco sauce, salt, and pepper. Beat vigorously for 1-2 seconds with a wire whisk or electric mixer. Add oil gradually and continue beating with whisk or mixer until all of oil has been added. Add more salt to taste, if necessary; add lemon juice, if desired. Add parsley, onion, pickles, and capers; blend well. (Makes 1½ cups sauce.)

Serves 6 or more.

*Florida Game and Fresh Water Fish Commission*

# Meats

## Walter's Special Tenderloin

*Whole beef tenderloin (about 6 pounds)*
*Spice Islands seasoned tenderizer*
*French's Worcestershire sauce*

Remove all fat and gristle from tenderloin. Sprinkle tenderizer liberally on all surfaces of tenderloin, then prick meat all over with sharp-tined fork. Let meat sit at room temperature for 1 hour or more. To cook on a gas grill, sear meat on high heat for 3 minutes on each side. Apply Worcestershire sauce liberally, then cook on high heat for 6-7 minutes on each side. Let stand for at least 10 minutes before slicing like a London broil.

NOTE: I cook the tenderloin in a wire grill basket—this makes it easy to turn over.

*Walter B. Arnold, Jr., Miami*

## Spicy Pot Roast

*½ teaspoon pepper*
*½ teaspoon ground cloves*
*½ teaspoon mace*
*½ teaspoon allspice*
*1 tablespoon salt*
*1 (4-pound) bone-in beef rump roast*
*½ cup water*
*1 medium onion, chopped*
*2 cloves garlic, chopped*
*¼ cup salad oil*
*2 tablespoons lime juice*
*2 to 3 tablespoons vinegar*

Combine pepper, cloves, mace, allspice, and salt; mix together. Rub spices into roast. Place roast in covered roasting pan; add water. Sprinkle onion and garlic over meat. In small bowl, combine salad oil, lime juice, and vinegar to make marinade; pour over meat. Marinate in refrigerator for 4 hours or longer. Cover and bake at 325°F for 4 hours or until meat is tender.

Serves 8.

*Florida Department of Agriculture and Consumer Services*

# Light Beef Stroganoff

*1 pound lean, boneless round steak*
*½ cup chopped onion*
*1 clove garlic, minced*
*1 teaspoon reduced-calorie margarine*
*2 cups sliced fresh mushrooms*
*3 tablespoons dry red wine or sherry*
*1 tablespoon cornstarch*
*¾ cup beef broth*
*¼ teaspoon pepper*
*¼ teaspoon dried dill weed*
*8 ounces plain nonfat yogurt*
*2 tablespoons chopped fresh parsley*
*Hot cooked noodles*

Place round steak in freezer until partially frozen. Slice steak diagonally across the grain into 3x½-inch strips; set aside. In skillet, sauté onion and garlic in margarine until tender. Add steak and mushrooms; cook, stirring constantly, until steak is browned. Add wine; cover and simmer for 10 minutes. In small bowl, dissolve cornstarch in broth. Stir cornstarch into beef mixture; cook, stirring constantly, until smooth and thickened. Remove from heat; stir in pepper, dill weed, and yogurt. Toss parsley with noodles. Serve beef mixture over noodles.

Serves 4.

NOTE: This recipe is a low-fat version of a traditionally high-fat favorite. Nutritional information per serving: 291 calories, 110 mg cholesterol, 267 mg sodium, 8 g fat.

*Florida Beef Council*

# Walter's Devilburgers

*Ground beef (chuck is good)*

**TO EACH POUND OF GROUND BEEF, ADD:**

*3 tablespoons catsup*
*1 teaspoon prepared mustard*
*1 teaspoon salt*
*Dash of pepper*
*Chopped onion to taste*
*French's Worcestershire sauce*

Combine ground beef with catsup, mustard, salt, pepper, and onion; mix thoroughly. Form mixture into burgers. To cook on a gas grill, sear burgers on high heat for 2 minutes on each side. Douse liberally with Worcestershire sauce, then cook for 4 minutes on each side. Serve burgers on buns, if desired.

NOTE: We use three pounds of ground beef at a time. Also, we use a wire grill basket—you can get twelve burgers in at a time, and it's easy to turn.

*Walter B. Arnold, Jr., Miami*

# Pork Loin Roulade

*4 boneless center pork loin slices (about 1 pound)*
*½ red bell pepper, cut into strips*
*½ green pepper, cut into strips*
*1 tablespoon cooking oil*
*⅔ cup orange juice*
*⅔ cup bottled barbecue sauce*
*1 tablespoon prepared Dijon-style mustard*

Place pork cutlets between two pieces of clear plastic wrap; pound with a mallet to about ¼-inch thickness. Place several red and green pepper strips crosswise on each cutlet, then roll up jelly-roll style. Secure rolls with wooden toothpicks. In large heavy skillet, brown pork rolls in hot cooking oil. Drain fat from skillet. With pork rolls still in skillet, add orange juice, barbecue sauce, and mustard; bring mixture to boil. Reduce heat; cover and simmer for 10-12 minutes or until pork is tender. Remove toothpicks from rolls before serving.

Serves 4 (255 calories per serving).

*National Pork Producers Council*

# Sweet-and-Sour Pork Loin

*1 (4- to 5-pound) boneless loin pork roast*
*1 cup brown sugar, packed*
*¾ cup teriyaki sauce*
*¾ cup dry red wine*
*¾ cup chili sauce*
*½ teaspoon ground cloves*
*¼ teaspoon pepper*
*⅛ teaspoon garlic powder*

Place pork roast in plastic bag. Combine all remaining ingredients to make marinade; mix well. Pour marinade over roast in bag; close bag and tie securely. Place roast in a shallow baking dish; marinate in refrigerator for 8-24 hours.

When ready to cook roast, prepare covered grill, positioning drip pan in center and banking medium-hot coals. Remove roast from plastic bag; place roast on center of grill. Grill until meat thermometer registers 165°F, about 1½ to 2 hours. Brush roast occasionally with marinade while cooking. Let roast stand for at least 10 minutes before carving.

Serves 12-15 (293 calories per serving).

*National Pork Producers Council*

## Javanese Pork Sate

*1 pound lean boneless pork*
*2 tablespoons peanut butter*
*½ cup minced onion*
*1 clove garlic, minced*
*2 tablespoons lemon juice*
*2 tablespoons soy sauce*
*1 tablespoon brown sugar*
*Dash of hot pepper sauce*
*1 tablespoon cooking oil*

Cut pork into ½-inch cubes. Combine all remaining ingredients in blender container; blend to mix well. Pour mixture over pork and marinate for 10 minutes. Thread pork cubes on skewers. (If using bamboo skewers, first soak skewers in water for 1 hour to prevent burning.) Grill or broil skewered pork for 10-12 minutes, turning occasionally, until done. Serve with hot cooked rice, if desired.

Serves 4 (270 calories per serving).

*National Pork Producers Council*

## Italian Pork Chops

*6 center-cut pork chops, ¾ inch thick*
*½ cup bread crumbs*
*2 teaspoons Italian seasoning*
*3 tablespoons grated Parmesan cheese*
*1 teaspoon salt*
*⅛ teaspoon pepper*
*1 egg, well beaten*
*¼ cup water*
*½ cup all-purpose flour*
*¼ cup olive oil*
*1 (8-ounce) can tomato sauce*
*6 slices mozzarella cheese*

Preheat oven to 325°F.

Remove bone from each pork chop; place each chop on a piece of waxed paper and flatten, using a rolling pin or meat mallet. In small mixing bowl, combine bread crumbs, Italian seasoning, Parmesan cheese, salt, and pepper; set aside. In another bowl, mix egg and water. Dredge each chop in flour, then dip in egg mixture, and then dredge in bread-crumb mixture. In large skillet, sauté chops in hot olive oil until browned. Place chops in three-quart shallow baking dish; spoon half of the tomato sauce over chops. Bake at 325°F for 20-30 minutes. Remove from oven; place a slice of cheese on each chop and spoon remaining tomato sauce on top. Return to oven for 10 additional minutes.

Serves 6.

*Florida Department of Agriculture and Consumer Services*

# Pork Chops and Sweet Potatoes

*Salt and pepper to taste*
*¾ cup all-purpose flour*
*4 loin or rib pork chops, cut ¾ to 1 inch*
*    thick*
*2 tablespoons cooking oil*
*3 to 4 sweet potatoes, cooked, peeled*
*    and cut into pieces*

**SAUCE**

*2 tablespoons margarine or butter*
*½ cup currant jelly*
*½ cup orange juice*
*1 tablespoon lemon juice*
*Rind of 1 lemon, grated*
*1 teaspoon dry mustard*
*1 teaspoon paprika*
*½ teaspoon ground ginger*

In a shallow pan, combine salt, pepper, and flour. Dredge chops in flour mixture, then brown in hot oil in frying pan. In saucepan, combine all sauce ingredients, mixing well; simmer for 3 minutes. Arrange pork chops and sweet potatoes in a shallow baking dish. Pour ¾ cup of the sauce over chops and potatoes; bake, uncovered, at 350°F for 40-45 minutes. Baste with remaining sauce while baking.

Serves 4.

*National Pork Producers Council*

# Orange-Glazed Barbecued Spareribs

*4 (3-pound) racks of ribs*

**BARBECUE SAUCE**

*6 large oranges*
*Juice from 2 lemons*
*1 quart catsup*
*½ cup cider vinegar*
*½ cup prepared mustard*
*2 cups brown sugar*
*1 cup Worcestershire sauce*
*½ teaspoon garlic powder*
*1½ teaspoons celery salt*
*½ teaspoon black pepper*
*¼ teaspoon cayenne pepper*
*Dill pickle juice or water (optional)*

Bake ribs in slow oven (325°F) for 45 minutes. Drain off grease; pour Barbecue Sauce over ribs and continue baking until done, turning ribs in sauce every 5 minutes.

To make Barbecue Sauce: Grate peel from two oranges; squeeze juice from all six oranges. Combine orange peel and juice with all remaining ingredients. Thin sauce with dill pickle juice or water, if desired.

Serves 12 as an appetizer, 6 for dinner.

*Florida Department of Citrus*

# Swiss-Fried Venison Steak

*1 pound venison steak, one inch thick*
*¼ cup flour*
*1 teaspoon salt*
*¼ teaspoon pepper*
*3 tablespoons fat or cooking oil*
*3 tablespoons chopped onion*
*3 tablespoons tomato sauce or catsup*
*1 cup water*

Pat steak dry with paper towels. Pound flour onto both sides of meat, then sprinkle with salt and pepper. In frying pan, heat fat or oil; brown steak on both sides. Add onion, tomato sauce, and water. Cover and boil for 3 minutes, then bake at 325°F for 1 hour, basting steak often.

*Florida Game and Fresh Water Fish Commission*

# Barbecued Venison Roast

*1 (3- to 4-pound) boneless venison roast*
*2 envelopes onion soup mix*
*1 cup salad oil*
*½ cup cider vinegar*
*2 tablespoons brown sugar*
*2 tablespoons Worcestershire sauce*
*1 cup catsup*

Trim all fat from roast; place roast in glass dish. In small bowl, combine soup mix, oil, vinegar, brown sugar, and Worcestershire sauce to make marinade; mix well. Pour marinade over roast; cover and refrigerate overnight. To cook, transfer roast and marinade to roaster; stir in catsup. Bake at 300°F for 4 hours. Serve with sauce. Slice leftover roast thinly and serve on sesame-seed buns with sauce.

*Liz Windham*
*Division of Wildlife*
*Panama City Regional Office*

# One-Dish Meals

## Country Cabbage Casserole

1 pound ground chuck
1 green pepper, chopped
1 large sweet onion, chopped
1 (8-ounce) can mushrooms, drained
½ head cabbage, chopped
1 box instant Uncle Ben's wild rice
1 box Jiffy corn bread mix
Salt and pepper to taste

In skillet, combine ground chuck, green pepper, onion, and mushrooms; cook until done, then drain and set aside. Boil cabbage until done; drain and set aside. Prepare wild rice according to package directions. Prepare corn bread batter according to package directions, but do not bake. In large baking dish, layer ingredients in the following order: meat mixture (seasoned to taste), cabbage (seasoned to taste), and rice; pour corn bread batter over top. Bake at 350°F until corn bread is golden brown, about 25-30 minutes.

Serves 4-5.

*Phyllis Bridges, Mango*

## Taco Casserole

1 pound ground beef
1 cup chopped onion
1 package taco seasoning mix
1 (8-ounce) jar taco sauce
3 cups regular-size corn chips, broken
1 (15½-ounce) can kidney beans, drained
1½ cups grated sharp cheddar cheese
2 cups shredded lettuce
1 cup chopped ripe tomatoes

In large skillet, brown ground beef and onions; drain off all but ¼ cup drippings. Add taco seasoning mix and taco sauce to meat mixture; mix well. Place half of the corn chips in a two-quart casserole; top with meat mixture, then kidney beans. Cover and bake at 350°F for 25 minutes. Uncover casserole; top with cheddar cheese and remaining corn chips. Return to oven for an additional 5 minutes. Before serving, top casserole with shredded lettuce and chopped tomatoes.

Serves 4-5.

*Florida Department of Agriculture and Consumer Services*

# Working Woman's Delight

1 pound ground beef
Salt, pepper, and garlic salt to taste
½ cup grated sharp cheddar cheese
1 bag frozen oriental vegetables
1 can cream of mushroom soup
1 bag Tater Tots

Mix ground beef with salt, pepper, and garlic salt; press into the bottom of a baking pan. Sprinkle half of the cheese over raw hamburger, then sprinkle vegetables over cheese. Season with salt and pepper to taste. Spread undiluted soup over vegetables, then sprinkle remainder of cheese over soup. Top with Tater Tots. Bake at 325°F for 45 minutes to 1 hour.

Serves 6.

*Phyllis Bridges, Mango*

# Pastichio

1 pound rigatoni macaroni
1 small onion, chopped
1½ pounds ground chuck
Small amount of oil
1 can tomato paste
1 (6-ounce) can tomato sauce
3 eggs
⅔ cup grated Parmesan cheese
1 cup (2 sticks) butter or margarine
⅔ cup flour
1 quart milk

Cook macaroni according to package directions; drain, then set aside. In skillet, brown onion and ground chuck in oil. Add tomato paste and tomato sauce; blend well, then cover and set aside. In small bowl, beat eggs; stir in cheese, then set aside. Melt butter in large saucepan; stir in flour, then gradually stir in milk. Cook over medium heat until thick, stirring constantly. Add egg-cheese mixture to sauce in saucepan, then stir sauce into macaroni. Spoon half of the macaroni mixture into an 8½x13-inch pan. Spoon all of the meat mixture over the macaroni, then spoon remaining macaroni mixture on top of meat. Bake uncovered at 350°F for 30-45 minutes. Let cool for about 15 minutes before serving.

Serves 6-8.

*Pinellas County Cooperative Extension Service, Largo*

# Stuffed Grape Leaves
## (Dolmathes)

2 jars grape leaves
Boiling water
1 large onion, chopped
4 tablespoons butter, divided
1½ pounds ground lamb
½ cup cooked rice
1 (8-ounce) can tomato sauce
Salt and pepper to taste
2 cups water

**EGG-LEMON SAUCE**

4 eggs
2 tablespoons water
Juice of 2 lemons
2 cups liquid (from cooked dolmathes)

Steam grape leaves in boiling water to remove brine and to soften them a little. Rinse in cool water; drain and set aside. In skillet, sauté onion in two tablespoons butter until soft and transparent but not brown. In mixing bowl, combine cooked onion with ground lamb, rice, tomato sauce, salt, and pepper; mix well.

Arrange a few grape leaves over the bottom of a large pot; set aside. Place one large grape leaf (or two small grape leaves) on a flat surface, then place about one tablespoon of the meat mixture in the center of the leaf. Fold sides of leaf over meat, then roll to seal. Continue stuffing remaining grape leaves with meat mixture until all meat is used. Arrange rolled grape leaves side by side in pot. Add water and remaining two tablespoons butter. Cover with heatproof plate and lid. Simmer over low heat for about 30 minutes or until done. Serve plain or with Egg-Lemon Sauce.

To make Egg-Lemon Sauce: In mixing bowl, combine eggs and water; beat until light and fluffy. Add lemon juice slowly, beating continuously. Carefully drain liquid from pot containing cooked dolmathes; add water to liquid to make two cups, if necessary. Add hot liquid to egg-lemon juice mixture, stirring as you pour. Pour sauce over dolmathes. Allow to sit for about 15 minutes before serving. Serve hot.

*Pinellas County Cooperative Extension Service, Largo*

# Oriental Rice à la Egg Roll

*3 cups cooked brown rice*
*1 (2-ounce) jar pimientos, chopped*
*½ cup pine nuts or slivered almonds,*
  *toasted*
*½ cup chopped green pepper*
*1 bunch green onions, diced*
*2 to 4 tablespoons soy sauce*
*1 (8-ounce) can bamboo shoots, cut in*
  *halves*

**EGG ROLL**

*6 eggs, beaten well*
*5 tablespoons biscuit mix*
*4 tablespoons water*
*Salt and pepper to taste*

Preheat oven to 350°F.

In mixing bowl, combine rice, pimientos, nuts, green pepper, green onions, soy sauce, and bamboo shoots; toss together lightly. Spoon rice mixture into buttered two-quart baking dish; bake at 350°F for 30 minutes.

To make Egg Roll: Line jelly-roll pan with foil; spray foil with nonstick cooking spray. To preheat pan, place in 350°F oven for about 3 minutes. In mixing bowl, combine eggs, biscuit mix, water, salt, and pepper; mix well. Pour egg mixture into preheated foil-lined pan. Bake at 350°F for about 15 minutes or until eggs are dry on top. Remove pan from oven immediately. Take edges of foil and lift egg roll out of pan. Roll up egg roll in jelly-roll style; allow to cool for a few minutes, then unroll. Spread about one-quarter or one-third of the rice mixture on top of egg roll, then roll up egg roll again in jelly-roll style. To serve, place egg roll in center of serving platter and surround with remaining oriental rice mixture. Garnish as desired.

Serves 4-5.

*Cindy Rountree, Jacksonville*
*Florida Egg Cooking Contest Finalist*

# Etah's Fried Rice

3 tablespoons cooking oil
1 large onion, chopped
½ cup stuffed Spanish olives, sliced
1 cup cooked Uncle Ben's converted rice
1 cup cooked shrimp
1 cup chopped cooked ham or seasoned
   pork
1 cup chopped smoked sausage
1 tablespoon Italian seasoning
1 tablespoon Cajun seasoning
Garlic salt to taste

Heat oil in large skillet; sauté onion in oil until tender. Add olives, rice, shrimp, ham or pork, and sausage; mix well. Sprinkle with seasonings. Stir-fry for 15-20 minutes or until mixture is well blended and rice is slightly brown but not hard.

Serves 4.

NOTE: Delicious served with a tossed salad and hot bread. Enjoy.

*Etah Garcia, Tampa*

# VEGETABLES

# Broccoli Supreme

1 (10-ounce) package frozen chopped
  broccoli
1 can cream of mushroom soup
1 cup mayonnaise
2 eggs, beaten
1 cup grated sharp cheese
2 tablespoons minced onion
½ cup crushed Ritz crackers (optional)

Cook broccoli according to package directions; drain well. Combine soup, mayonnaise, eggs, cheese, and onion; mix well. Pour soup mixture over broccoli and stir. Place broccoli mixture in baking dish; sprinkle top with crushed crackers, if desired. Bake uncovered at 350°F for 30 minutes or until bubbling hot.

Serves 6-8.

NOTE: I have doubled the amount of broccoli, and I have also used cream of chicken soup in place of the cream of mushroom soup. This dish is delicious any way.

*Gloria Cuyler, Inverness*

# Sunshine Carrots

5 medium carrots, peeled, trimmed and
  sliced
1 tablespoon sugar
1 teaspoon cornstarch
¼ teaspoon salt
½ teaspoon ground ginger
¼ cup orange juice
1 tablespoon butter or corn-oil
  margarine

Cook carrots until tender, approximately 15 minutes; set aside and keep warm. In small saucepan, combine sugar, cornstarch, salt, and ginger; add orange juice and cook, stirring constantly, until mixture thickens. Boil for 1 minute. Stir in butter. Pour over hot carrots and toss to coat.

Serves 4.

*Racine A. Daniels, Naples*

# Savory Eggplant Casserole
## (Microwave Recipe)

1 medium eggplant, peeled and cubed
Water
1 egg, slightly beaten
½ cup evaporated milk
1 cup dry bread crumbs
½ teaspoon sage
½ teaspoon parsley flakes
½ teaspoon oregano
½ teaspoon pepper
½ teaspoon salt
2 tablespoons minced onion
1 cup shredded cheddar cheese

Place eggplant cubes in two-quart glass casserole; add enough water to cover eggplant. Cover casserole and microwave on High for 8 minutes, stirring once. Drain eggplant, then mash. Mix eggplant with all remaining ingredients, reserving ½ cup shredded cheese. Place mixture in 1½-quart covered casserole. Microwave on High for 6 minutes, stirring and turning dish every 2 minutes. Sprinkle remaining cheese across top of casserole; microwave for 1 additional minute.

Serves 6-8.

*Florida Department of Agriculture and Consumer Services*

# Green Beans Oriental

¼ cup vegetable oil
2 cups green beans, cut into one-inch
    pieces
½ small onion, sliced diagonally
1 cup thinly sliced fresh mushrooms
1 (10-ounce) can water chestnuts, sliced
¼ cup roasted peanuts
⅓ cup oriental sauce or soy sauce
1 tablespoon toasted sesame seeds

Heat oil in wok or electric skillet to 375°F. Add green beans and stir-fry for 3 minutes. Add onion and mushrooms; stir-fry for 3 additional minutes. Add all remaining ingredients except sesame seeds, stirring until mixture is heated thoroughly and sauce thickens. Sprinkle with toasted sesame seeds before serving.

Serves 4.

*Florida Department of Agriculture and Consumer Services*

# Cheesy Potato Scallop

6 cups thinly sliced, cooked new
  potatoes
2 small onions, sliced and separated
  into rings
1 teaspoon salt
¼ teaspoon pepper
2 cups cottage cheese
1 cup dairy sour cream
1½ cups shredded cheddar cheese
Paprika

In a buttered two-quart casserole, alternate layers of potatoes and onions, sprinkling potatoes with salt and pepper as you layer. Combine cottage cheese and sour cream; spoon over potatoes. Top with cheddar cheese, then sprinkle with paprika. Bake at 350°F for 20 minutes.

Serves 8.

*Florida Department of Agriculture and Consumer Services*

*Good. Jean Green's recipe in new Presbyterian*

# Potato Casserole

1 (8-ounce) carton dairy sour cream
2 cans cream of potato soup
12 ounces cream cheese, softened
¾ cup (1½ sticks) margarine, melted
1 (32-ounce) package frozen hash
  browns, partially thawed

In large bowl, combine sour cream, soup, cream cheese, and margarine; mix together well. Stir in hash browns. Pour mixture into greased 13x9x2-inch pan. (Casserole can be frozen at this stage, if desired; thaw for one day in refrigerator before baking.) Bake at 350°F for 40-50 minutes.

Serves 10-12.

NOTE: This is one of my "regular" dishes for "champagne breakfast."

*Paula P. Stanley, Inverness
Extension Home Economics Agent*

# Yellow Summer Squash Casserole

*3 pounds yellow squash*
*1 (16-ounce) package grated sharp*
*   cheddar cheese (reserve a small*
*   amount for top of casserole)*
*1 egg*
*1 can cream of mushroom soup*
*1 large onion, diced*
*1 teaspoon garlic salt*
*½ cup dairy sour cream*
*Salt and pepper to taste*
*1 (9-ounce) package bread crumbs*

Cut up squash; cook until tender, then drain. Place squash in casserole dish; set aside. Mix together all remaining ingredients except bread crumbs. Pour soup mixture over squash in casserole dish; mix together. Sprinkle bread crumbs on top of squash mixture, then top with reserved cheese. Bake at 350°F for 30 minutes.

Serves 10.

*Mrs. William O. Higgins, Tampa*

# Cheesy Florida Vegetable Medley

*2 strips bacon, cut into small pieces*
*¾ cup chopped fresh onion*
*4 medium ears fresh corn*
*2 medium zucchini, cut into ½-inch*
*   slices*
*1½ teaspoons ground cumin*
*¾ teaspoon salt*
*¼ teaspoon garlic powder*
*3 medium tomatoes, cut into wedges*
*1 cup (4 ounces) grated cheddar cheese*
*   (optional)*

In large skillet, cook bacon until crisp. Pour off all bacon fat except one teaspoon; add onion to skillet and cook until tender. Remove husks and silks from corn; rinse corn. Using a sharp knife, cut corn kernels from cobs. Add corn, zucchini, cumin, salt, and garlic powder to mixture in skillet; mix well. Cover pan and cook for about 15 minutes or until zucchini is tender. Add tomatoes; heat through. Turn vegetables into serving dish; sprinkle with cheese, if desired.

Serves 6.

NOTE: Each serving provides: With cheese—173 calories, 9 g protein, 19 g carbohydrates, 8 g fat. Without cheese—97 calories, 4 g protein, 19 g carbohydrates, 2 g fat.

*Florida Department of Agriculture and Consumer Services*

# PICKLES & CONDIMENTS

 ## Sherri's Bread-and-Butter Pickles

6 pounds pickling cucumbers
2 or 3 large onions
⅓ cup pickling salt
Ice cubes, crushed
3 cups sugar
3 cups cider vinegar
2 tablespoons mustard seed
2 teaspoons mixed pickling spice
½ teaspoon ground turmeric

Wash cucumbers; scrub gently with a brush to remove spines. Remove blossom fragments. Cut a thin slice from each end of cucumbers; discard ends. Cut cucumbers crosswise into ¼-inch slices, making about five quarts sliced cucumbers. Peel onions; cut in half top to bottom. Lay cut-side down, then cut crosswise into ¼-inch slices, making about one quart onion slices. Layer cucumber slices and onion slices alternately in a large pot or bowl, sprinkling some of the pickling salt over each layer. Cover with crushed ice cubes, then place lid on pot or bowl; let stand for 3 hours.

Wash eight pint jars in hot, soapy water; rinse well. Keep jars in hot water until needed. Prepare lids as manufacturer directs. Place cucumber mixture in a colander to drain; rinse well with cold water. In an eight-quart pot, combine sugar, vinegar, mustard seed, pickling spice, and turmeric. Bring vinegar mixture to boil over medium-high heat; boil for 5 minutes. Add drained cucumbers and onions; return to boil. Remove from heat. Pack hot cucumber mixture into hot jars, leaving ¼-inch head space. Add enough vinegar mixture to each jar to cover cucumbers. Release trapped air by running a knife around the inside of each jar. Wipe rims of jars with a clean damp cloth. Seal jars. Adjust caps. Process for 15 minutes in boiling water bath.

Makes 8 pints.

NOTE: Make sure you use cucumbers that have not been waxed. Use cucumbers less than twenty-four hours old.

*Sherri K. Vollick, Plant City*

## Crispy Sweet Pickle Chips

6 pounds pickling cucumbers (each
   three to four inches long)
3 cups Heinz distilled white vinegar
6 cups water
1½ cups granulated sugar
2 tablespoons pickling salt
2 tablespoons celery seed
2 tablespoons mustard seed

Wash cucumbers; cut crosswise into 1/3-inch slices. In large saucepan, combine cucumbers with all remaining ingredients; heat just to boiling. Pack hot cucumbers into clean, hot pint jars. Cover with boiling syrup, leaving ½-inch head space and making sure vinegar solution covers cucumbers. Seal jars at once. Adjust caps. Process for 5 minutes in boiling water bath.

Makes 4 to 5 pints.

NOTE: After sealing, let pickles stand for three or four days to enhance flavor.

*Sharon Johnson Townsend, Gainesville*

## Aunt Sharon's Sweet Pickles

4 pounds pickling cucumbers
4 cups water
2 cups vinegar
1 cup granulated sugar
2 tablespoons celery seed
2 tablespoons mustard seed
1 tablespoon pickling salt

Wash cucumbers; cut lengthwise into fourths. In large saucepan, combine cucumbers and all remaining ingredients; heat just to boiling. Pack hot cucumbers into clean, hot pint jars. Cover with boiling syrup, leaving ½-inch head space and making sure vinegar solution covers cucumbers. Seal each jar immediately. Adjust caps. Process for 5 minutes in boiling water bath.

Makes 4 to 5 pints.

NOTE: After sealing, let pickles stand for three or four days to enhance full flavor.

*Sharon Johnson Townsend, Gainesville*

# Watermelon Rind Pickles

Rind of 1 large or 2 small watermelons
Salt
Water
8 cups sugar
4 cups cider vinegar
2 tablespoons whole cloves
5 sticks cinnamon
2 tablespoons whole allspice

Peel and remove all green, red, and pink portions from watermelon rind. Cut white rind into one-inch cubes or slices. Cover rind with salt solution (¼ cup salt to each 4 cups water); let sit at room temperature overnight. The next day, drain thoroughly. Place rind in large pot and cover with cold water; heat and simmer until rind is almost tender, about 10 minutes. Drain thoroughly; set aside.

In large pot, combine sugar and vinegar. Tie cloves, cinnamon, and allspice in cheesecloth; add to vinegar mixture. Bring to boil and simmer, uncovered, for 5 minutes. Remove from heat; cool for about 15 minutes. Add drained watermelon rind to vinegar mixture; simmer until rind is clear and translucent, about 10-12 minutes. Discard spice bag. Immediately pack hot mixture into clean, hot pint jars, leaving ⅛-inch head space. Seal jars immediately. Adjust caps. Process for 5 minutes in boiling water bath.

Makes 4 pints.

NOTE: I like to put a piece of cinnamon stick and clove in each jar for added flavor.

*Ginny Polak, Tampa*

##  Pickled Miniature Corn

4 pounds miniature baby corn
3 cups water
3 cups white distilled vinegar
1 tablespoon salt
1 tablespoon dill seed

Wash and drain corn. In large pot, combine corn with all remaining ingredients; bring to boil. Pack hot corn into hot sterilized pint jars, leaving ¼-inch head space. Pour hot vinegar into jars to cover corn. Seal jars at once. Adjust caps. Process for 5 minutes in boiling water bath.

Makes 4 pints.

*Sharon Johnson Townsend, Gainesville*

## Pickled Pepper Strips

4 green bell peppers
4 yellow bell peppers
4 red bell peppers
3 whole garlic cloves, peeled
4 cups white vinegar
2 cups sugar
1 teaspoon freshly grated horseradish

Wash and seed peppers; cut into 1/3-inch strips. Pack pepper strips, alternating colors, into three sterilized pint jars. Place one garlic clove in each jar. In saucepan, combine vinegar and sugar; bring to boil. Pour hot vinegar over peppers in jars, leaving ½-inch head space. Divide horseradish equally among jars. Seal jars with sterilized seals and lids. Adjust caps. Process for 10 minutes in boiling water bath. After jars are sealed, store in a cool dark place. Age at least 30 days before serving.

Makes 3 pints.

NOTE: This recipe won Best of Show honors at the 1989 Florida State Fair and at the 1985 Pinellas County Fair.

*Shirley J. Myrsiades, Clearwater*

## Chow Chow Relish

2 quarts chopped cabbage (1 medium
    head)
1½ pounds onions, chopped (6 to 8
    medium onions)
6 medium green peppers, coarsely
    chopped
6 medium sweet red peppers, coarsely
    chopped
1 quart chopped green tomatoes (about
    1½ pounds)
¼ cup pickling salt
2 tablespoons Heinz mild mustard
6 cups Heinz distilled white vinegar
2½ cups granulated sugar
2 tablespoons mustard seed
1 tablespoon celery seed
1 tablespoon mixed pickling spice
1½ teaspoons ground turmeric
1½ teaspoons ground ginger

In large crock or nonmetallic container, combine cabbage, onions, green peppers, red peppers, green tomatoes, and pickling salt. Cover and let stand overnight. The next morning, drain vegetables; rinse, then drain again. Set vegetables aside.

In large saucepan, blend mustard with a little vinegar; add remaining vinegar, sugar, and all spices. Simmer vinegar mixture for 20 minutes. Add drained vegetables and simmer for 10 minutes, stirring occasionally. Continue simmering while quickly packing hot mixture into clean, hot pint jars. Fill each jar within ½ inch of top, making sure vinegar solution covers vegetables. Seal jars at once. Adjust caps. Process for 5 minutes in boiling water bath.

Makes 6 to 8 pints.

*Sharon Johnson Townsend, Gainesville*

## Zucchini Relish

10 cups grated zucchini
4 onions, chopped
3 tablespoons salt
2 red bell peppers, grated
2 green bell peppers, grated
2¼ cups vinegar
4 cups sugar
1 teaspoon cornstarch
1 teaspoon nutmeg
1 teaspoon turmeric
1 teaspoon dry mustard
1 teaspoon celery seed

In large crock or container, combine zucchini, onions, and salt; mix well. Let stand overnight. The next day, drain zucchini and onions. In large pot, combine zucchini and onions with all remaining ingredients. Bring mixture to boil; boil for 30 minutes, stirring occasionally. Pack mixture into prepared pint jars. Seal. Adjust caps. Process for 5 minutes in boiling water bath.

Makes 5 pints.

*Victoria Mowrey, Tampa*

 ## Chunky Applesauce

20 large apples
4 cups water
2½ cups sugar

Wash apples; quarter, core, and remove all bruised or decayed parts of fruit. (If peeled fruit is to stand several minutes before cooking, drop into prepared solution to prevent discoloration; drain before cooking.) In large pot, combine apples with water and sugar; cook on low heat until apples are soft, about 30 minutes. Remove from heat. Beat mixture at medium speed of electric mixer for 1-2 minutes. Pack hot mixture into hot sterilized pint jars, leaving ½-inch head space. Put on lids and screw bands firmly tight. Adjust caps. Process for 15 minutes in boiling water bath.

Makes about 4 pints.

*Sharon Johnson Townsend, Gainesville*

 ## Spiced Cranberries

1⅓ cups distilled white vinegar
⅔ cup water
4 cups granulated sugar
4 teaspoons ground ginger
1 teaspoon ground cloves
2 pounds fresh cranberries, washed
  (2 quarts)

In large saucepan, combine vinegar, water, sugar, ginger, and cloves; bring to boil. Add cranberries; simmer for 25 minutes, stirring occasionally. (As berries simmer, they will pop.) Continue simmering while quickly packing mixture into clean, hot pint jars. Fill each jar within ½ inch of top, making sure vinegar solution covers cranberries. Seal each jar at once. Adjust caps. Process for 5 minutes in boiling water bath.

Makes 4 pints.

NOTE: Serve cold as a relish or "fruity vegetable," or warmed slightly to use as a sauce/glaze for meat or fowl.

*Eleanor C. Lynch, Tampa*

 ## Cranberry Chutney

¾ cup sugar
1 cup water
4 cups fresh cranberries
1 cup golden raisins
½ cup red wine vinegar
1½ tablespoons curry powder
2 tablespoons molasses
2 teaspoons powdered ginger
1 tablespoon Worcestershire sauce
1 teaspoon salt
½ teaspoon hot pepper sauce
1 cup walnuts
2 tablespoons grated orange rind
   (optional)

In medium saucepan, combine sugar and water; bring to boil, then reduce heat and simmer for 5 minutes. Add cranberries; cook just until skins pop, about 5 minutes. Stir in all remaining ingredients except walnuts and orange rind; simmer uncovered for 15 minutes or until mixture thickens, stirring occasionally. During last 5 minutes, add walnuts and orange rind. Ladle hot mixture into hot sterilized pint jars. Seal at once. Adjust caps. Process for 5 minutes in boiling water bath.

Makes 2 pints.

NOTE: Serve cold as a relish or "fruity vegetable"—very good with turkey, chicken, or ham.

*Eleanor C. Lynch, Tampa*

## Carambola Papaya Chutney

1 cup carambola* star-slices (slightly
   green on the ribs)
3 cups papaya cubes (fully ripe)
1 onion, sliced
½ cup freshly squeezed lime juice
¼ cup white vinegar
½ cup chopped walnuts
½ cup seedless golden raisins
3 cups sugar
1 teaspoon ground ginger
¼ red pepper pod (add only if hot
   chutney is desired)

In large saucepan, combine all ingredients. Bring mixture to boil, stirring constantly; boil for 10 minutes. Remove from heat; cool to room temperature. Chill for 24 hours or overnight to blend flavors. The next day, bring chutney to boil. Ladle hot mixture into hot prepared jars. Seal with lids and caps. Adjust caps. Process in boiling water bath for 10 minutes. Cool. Label jars before storing.

*NOTE: Often called "star fruit," the carambola earned its name from its star-shaped slices when cut into cross-sections. Select firm, shiny-skinned fruit and allow to ripen at room temperature.

*Nan Brooks, Homestead*

## ❀ Dried Dill

*Use fresh dill left over from the garden or that you have bought and are unable to use otherwise.*

Wash dill thoroughly; pat dry with paper towels. Let sit for a while to be sure it is good and dry. Cut heads and stalks into equal lengths. Place dill on microwave-safe plate. Microwave on High for about 3 minutes, depending on amount of dill and your microwave. When dill is dried, place in airtight jars until needed for seasoning.

Preparation time: 10 minutes

*Jeanne B. Mathews, Lutz*

## ❀ Autumn's Purple Onion Chips

Select 3- to 3½-inch purple onions with the darkest skins (these tend to have well-defined rings that enhance the appearance of the finished product). Peel onions and remove outermost fleshy layer. Cut off root area and discard for compost. Rinse onions well; slice into uniform ¼-inch slices, keeping the rings together.

Wipe trays/racks with a paper towel lightly sprayed with nonstick cooking spray. Arrange onion slices in a single layer on trays. Place trays in dehydrator or in oven at 130°F-150°F, with the oven door open several inches. Rotate trays, top to bottom and front to back, to encourage even drying. Check often and watch for scorching, which will ruin the flavor. Flip slices over every hour, keeping the rings intact.

Stop drying when texture is leathery to brittle, about 2-3 hours. Set trays in a dry place and allow to cool completely. Place cooled onions in clean, airtight containers; seal, label, and date containers. Store in a cool, dry, dark place. Onions will last for six months to one year—or until your family finds where they are hidden! Use as nutritious snacks or in recipes (allow to rehydrate in sauces). Enjoy!

### DRYING FOOD

Drying food is one of the oldest forms of food preservation—and one of the easiest and most economical. Dried or dehydrated food requires less space (one-third to one-half original size), needs no refrigeration (lasts up to one year), and has concentrated nutrients and flavor.

To dehydrate food, you must control temperature and air circulation to prevent spoiling. There are many methods to use, but oven drying or using a dehydrator are the best. Sun drying is possible, but not very practical in Florida due to the high

(Continued)

humidity and unpredictable rain, not to mention the critters eager for a tray of tidbits!

Oven drying can be done anytime, day or night, rain or shine. Use oven settings between 130°F-150°F. This is usually the lowest setting, but double check with an oven thermometer. Place prepared food on trays or racks, and leave the oven door open a crack (two to six inches). Use a fan in the room for air circulation.

Using a dehydrator eliminates most of the guesswork for beginners. A dehydrator maintains low, even temperatures and circulates air continuously while drying. The units come with ventilated trays and are easy to care for.

## RECIPE FOR DRYING A BLUE-RIBBON SUCCESS

**FOOD SELECTION:** Choose fresh, ripe, unblemished fruits, vegetables, and herbs.

**PREPARATION:** Work with clean hands, utensils, and trays. Handle food gently, wash well, rinse, and pat dry. Place prepared foods in a single layer, nearly touching, on trays or racks.

> Fruit and Veggies: Remove pits/seeds; peel apples, pears, nectarines; cut into uniform, thin slices. Dry for approximately 12 to 24 hours or until leathery or brittle.

> Herbs: Remove stems after drying. Break or cut into pieces and dry for approximately 2 to 4 hours or until herbs crumble easily.

**STORING:** After completely cool, store dried foods in clean, airtight containers. Label and date containers. Place in a dry, cool, dark place as this extends the shelf life to six to twelve months (or up to two years in the freezer!).

**REHYDRATE:** Soak 1 cup dried food in 1½ cups water for 20-30 minutes, adding more water if necessary. Rehydrating is not necessary with herbs.

*Autumn Eve Balthazor, Tampa*

# PRESERVES & SPREADS

# Strawberry Jam

4 cups crushed strawberries
7 cups sugar
½ lemon, finely chopped
½ teaspoon margarine
1 (3-ounce) pouch Certo

Wash fruit; drain. Mash or crush berries; measure four cups crushed fruit. In large kettle, combine crushed berries with sugar and lemon; mix well. Bring mixture to boil; add margarine and boil hard for 1 minute, stirring constantly. Remove from heat and add Certo; stir well. Skim off any foam. (The margarine should help prevent foam.) Pour hot jam into sterilized jars. Seal. Adjust caps. Process for 15 minutes in boiling water bath.

Makes about 7 cups jam.

NOTE: It is always best to have some unripe fruit in with the ripe fruit—this is where most of the pectin is and it will help in setting up the jam.

*Jeanne B. Mathews, Lutz*

# Cranberry Port Jelly

2 cups cranberry juice cocktail
3½ cups sugar
1 (3-ounce) pouch liquid pectin
¼ cup Port wine

In large saucepan, combine cranberry juice cocktail and sugar; bring to full rolling boil, stirring constantly. Add pectin. Return to full, rolling boil; boil hard for 1 minute. Remove from heat; stir in Port wine. Skim off foam. Immediately ladle into hot sterilized jars, leaving ⅛-inch head space. Seal. Adjust caps. Process for 5 minutes in boiling water bath.

Makes 5 eight-ounce jars.

NOTE: This jelly has a beautiful color and makes a very pretty gift at Christmastime.

*Judy Marks, Valrico*

## Grapefruit-Pineapple Jelly

2¼ cups unsweetened grapefruit-
  pineapple juice
¾ cup water
1 (¾-ounce) box powdered pectin
3½ cups sugar

In large saucepan, combine juice and water. Stir in powdered pectin. Bring mixture to hard boil over high heat. Stir in sugar immediately, then return to boil. Boil hard for 30 seconds—time exactly; stir constantly. Remove from heat. Skim off foam. Pour mixture into clean, hot half-pint jars. Seal. Invert jars for 1-2 minutes while jelly is hot, then return jars to upright position and cool.

Makes 4 half-pints.

*Pat DePrez, New Port Richey*

## Orange-Pineapple Jelly

2¼ cups unsweetened orange-pineapple
  juice
¾ cup water
1 (¾-ounce) box powdered pectin
3½ cups sugar

In large saucepan, combine juice and water; stir in pectin. Bring to hard boil over high heat. Stir in sugar immediately, then return mixture to boil. Boil hard for 30 seconds—time exactly; stir constantly. Remove from heat. Skim off foam. Pour mixture into clean, hot half-pint jars. Seal. Invert jars for 1-2 minutes while jelly is hot, then return jars to upright position and cool.

Makes 4 half-pints.

NOTE: This jelly really has an aroma while cooking!

*Pat DePrez, New Port Richey*

# Peach Jelly

3½ *pounds ripe peaches*
1 *cup water*
1 *(¾-ounce) box powdered pectin*
4½ *cups sugar*

Peel peaches and remove pits. Crush fruit in large kettle. Add water to peaches; simmer uncovered for 10 minutes. Place fruit in jelly bag and squeeze out juice. Measure 3½ cups juice. In saucepan, combine juice with pectin; cook and stir over high heat until mixture comes to rolling boil. Stir in sugar, then return to rolling boil. Boil for 1 minute, stirring constantly. Remove from heat. Skim off foam. Pour mixture into hot sterilized pint jars, leaving ¼-inch head space. Seal. Adjust caps. Process jars for 10 minutes in boiling water bath.

Makes 2½ to 3 pints.

NOTE: This is a very smooth spread— deliciously different.

*Norma Bobbett, Lutz*

# Raisin-Apple Jelly

2 *cups bottled apple juice*
3½ *cups sugar*
½ *cup currants*
1 *(3-ounce) pouch liquid pectin*

Measure apple juice into large saucepan; add sugar. Bring mixture to boil. Add currants; return to full boil. Add pectin; boil hard for 1 minute. Remove from heat. Skim off foam. Quickly pour hot mixture into sterilized half-pint jars. Seal. Adjust caps. Process for 10 minutes in boiling water bath.

Makes 4 half-pints.

NOTE: This is very easy and quick—a good beginner's or child's recipe to start with.

*Jeanne B. Mathews, Lutz*

 # Cranberry-Orange Marmalade

2 oranges
1 lemon
3 cups water
1 pound cranberries (about 4 cups)
1 (¾-ounce) box powdered pectin
7 cups sugar

To prepare fruit: Peel oranges and lemon; remove and discard half of the white part of rinds. Finely chop or grind the remaining rinds. In large saucepan, combine chopped rinds and water; bring to boil. Cover and simmer for 20 minutes, stirring occasionally. Chop peeled oranges and lemon. Sort and wash fully ripe cranberries. Add oranges, lemon, and cranberries to rind mixture; cover and cook slowly for 10 additional minutes.

To make Marmalade: Measure six cups of prepared fruit into a large kettle. (Add water to make six cups, if necessary.) Add pectin; stir well. Place kettle on high heat and, stirring constantly, quickly bring mixture to a full boil with bubbles over the entire surface. Stir in sugar; return to a full rolling boil. Boil hard for 1 minute, stirring constantly. Remove from heat. Skim off foam. Pour hot mixture into prepared half-pint jars. Seal. Adjust caps. Process for 5 minutes in boiling water bath.

Makes 10 or 11 half-pints.

NOTE: This recipe may also be made with frozen cranberries if fresh ones are not available.

*Judy Marks, Valrico*

# Orange Marmalade

8 small oranges
2½ cups water
⅛ teaspoon baking soda
5 level cups sugar
½ cup lemon juice
1 box Sure-Jell pectin
½ teaspoon margarine

Wash and scald pint jars, lids, and bands. You will need a six- to eight-quart pot and a long-handled spoon to cook marmalade.

To prepare fruit: Remove rind in quarters from oranges. Scrape off and discard half of the white membrane. Thinly slice rinds. Finely chop oranges, saving juice. In saucepan, combine rinds with water and baking soda. Bring to full boil, then cover and simmer for 20 minutes, stirring occasionally. Add chopped oranges, including juice; cover and simmer for 10 additional minutes.

To make Marmalade: Measure sugar into a bowl; set aside. Measure 4½ cups cooked fruit and rind mixture; add lemon juice, then stir in Sure-Jell and margarine. In large pot, bring fruit mixture to a full rolling boil over high heat, stirring constantly. Quickly add sugar, then return to full rolling boil, stirring constantly. Continue boiling and stirring for 2 minutes. Remove from heat. Skim off any foam with a large metal spoon. Fill jars immediately, leaving ¼-inch head space. Wipe jar rims and threads. Cover quickly with lids that have been dipped in boiling water. Seal jars; screw on bands tightly. Invert jars for 5 minutes, then turn upright.

Makes 3 pints.

NOTE: While the fruit and rinds are boiling, the jars can be scalded and the sugar measured into a bowl. ReaLemon may be used in place of lemon juice. Date jar lids.

*Ellen R. Follett, Lakeland*

 ## Peach Preserves

3 pounds peaches, finely chopped
  (4 cups)
2 tablespoons lemon juice
1 (³/₄-ounce) package powdered pectin
5½ cups sugar

In large saucepan, combine peaches, lemon juice, and pectin. Bring mixture to rolling boil. Stir in sugar, then return to rolling boil. Boil hard for 1 minute, stirring constantly. Remove from heat. Skim off foam, if necessary. Pour hot mixture into hot sterilized jars, leaving ¼-inch head space. Seal. Adjust caps. Process for 5 minutes in boiling water bath.

Makes 6½ cups.

*Sharon Johnson Townsend, Gainesville*

 ## Strawberry Preserves

2 quarts strawberries (4 cups)
1 (³/₄-ounce) package powdered pectin
7 cups sugar

Crush strawberries, one layer at a time. Measure four cups berries into large saucepan; add pectin. Bring mixture to full rolling boil over high heat, stirring constantly. Add sugar, then return to rolling boil. Boil hard for 1 minute, stirring constantly. Pour hot mixture into hot half-pint jars. Seal. Adjust caps. Process for 10 minutes in boiling water bath.

Makes about 8 half-pints.

*Sharon Johnson Townsend, Gainesville*

 # Apple Butter

*3 pounds Golden Grimes apples (to make 8 cups apple pulp)*
*3 cups water*
*4 cups sugar*
*2 teaspoons ground cinnamon*
*¼ teaspoon ground cloves*

To prepare apples: Wash apples; remove stem and blossom ends, then cut apples into quarters. In large cooking pot, combine apples with water; simmer for 30 minutes. Extract juice. Press apple pulp through sieve or food mill. Measure eight cups of apple pulp.

To make Apple Butter: In large saucepan, combine apple pulp, sugar, cinnamon, and cloves. Cook, stirring frequently, until flavors are well blended and mixture reaches desired consistency. Pour hot mixture into hot pint jars, leaving ¼-inch head space. Seal. Adjust caps. Process pints for 10 minutes in boiling water bath.

Makes approximately 5 pints.

NOTE: When I do apples in the fall, I like to use the whole product. First, I make my applesauce; then I take the cores and peelings (thick peelings) and cook them down. I extract the juice and make jelly and, not wanting to be wasteful, I then use the pulp for apple butter. All three are delicious and different!

*Norma Bobbett, Lutz*

# BREADS

## Quick Breads

(Continued)

# Yeast Breads

# Quick Breads

## Banana Nut Bread
### Best of Show—Young American

½ cup shortening
½ cup sugar
3 tablespoons milk
2 cups flour
1 teaspoon baking soda
½ teaspoon salt
1 cup mashed bananas
1 teaspoon vanilla flavoring
½ cup crushed nuts

In large mixing bowl, combine shortening, sugar, and milk; cream together. Combine flour, baking soda, and salt. Add dry ingredients to creamed mixture alternately with bananas; mix well. Add vanilla, then stir in nuts; mix well. Do not overmix. Pour batter into well-greased and floured loaf pan. Bake at 350°F for 45 minutes.

*Kim Gallaher, Crystal River*

## Banana-Macadamia Nut Bread

2¼ cups all-purpose flour
¼ cup granulated sugar
¾ cup brown sugar, firmly packed
3½ teaspoons baking powder
½ teaspoon salt
1½ teaspoons ground cinnamon
1¼ cups mashed ripe bananas
⅓ cup milk
1 teaspoon vinegar
3 tablespoons vegetable oil
1 egg
1 cup macadamia nuts, chopped

Preheat oven to 350°F. Generously grease a 9x5-inch loaf pan; set aside.

In large bowl, combine all ingredients except nuts. Beat at medium speed of electric mixer for 30 seconds or until dry ingredients are just moistened. Stir in nuts. Spoon batter into greased pan. Bake at 350°F for 60-70 minutes or until wooden pick inserted in center comes out clean. Cool in pan on wire rack for 10 minutes, then remove from pan and cool completely on wire rack before slicing.

Makes 1 loaf.

*Laura York, Valrico*

# Chocolate Zucchini Bread

3 cups all-purpose flour, sifted
2 cups sugar
¼ teaspoon baking powder
1 teaspoon baking soda
½ teaspoon salt
1 teaspoon cinnamon
¼ cup unsweetened cocoa
3 eggs, beaten
2 cups zucchini squash, grated
1 cup vegetable oil
1 teaspoon vanilla
1 cup chopped pecans

Preheat oven to 325°F.

Combine flour, sugar, baking powder, soda, salt, cinnamon, and cocoa; sift together into large mixing bowl. In medium bowl, combine eggs, zucchini, oil, vanilla, and pecans. Stir zucchini mixture into flour mixture; blend thoroughly. Spread batter in two well-greased and floured 9x5x3-inch loaf pans. Bake at 325°F for 1 hour or until knife inserted in center of a loaf comes out clean. Cool. Wrap and store overnight for easier slicing.

Makes 2 loaves.

*Florida Department of Agriculture and Consumer Services*

 ## Poppy Seed Bread

3 eggs
2½ cups sugar
1½ cups milk
1¼ cups vegetable oil
1½ cups poppy seeds
1½ teaspoons baking powder
1½ teaspoons salt
1½ teaspoons vanilla
1½ teaspoons almond extract
3 cups flour

**GLAZE**

¾ cup sugar
¼ cup orange juice
½ teaspoon vanilla
½ teaspoon almond extract
2 tablespoons butter

In mixing bowl, beat eggs and sugar together. Add milk, vegetable oil, poppy seeds, baking powder, salt, vanilla, and almond extract; mix well. Blend in flour. Pour batter into two greased 8x5x3-inch loaf pans. Bake at 325°F for 1 hour. Cool for 5 minutes, then remove from pans. Pour glaze over loaves; collect run-off and continue pouring over loaves until most of liquid is absorbed.

To make Glaze: In saucepan, combine sugar, orange juice, vanilla, almond extract, and butter. Heat until sugar dissolves.

*Doris Swank, Naples*

 ## Zucchini Bread

3 cups all-purpose flour
1¼ cups sugar
1 teaspoon cinnamon
1 teaspoon salt
1 teaspoon baking powder
¾ teaspoon soda
2 cups shredded zucchini
1 cup pecans
1 cup raisins
3 eggs
1 cup oil
2 teaspoons vanilla

In mixing bowl, combine flour, sugar, cinnamon, salt, baking powder, and soda. Add zucchini, pecans, and raisins. In another bowl, beat eggs with oil; pour over flour mixture and stir until moist. Add vanilla; mix well. Pour batter into two greased loaf pans; bake at 350°F for 1 hour 15 minutes. Cool in pans for 30 minutes.

*Richard Rogers, St. Petersburg*

## Zucchini Bread

¾ cup egg substitute, beaten
¾ cup safflower oil
1 cup wheat germ
2½ cups grated zucchini
2 ripe bananas, mashed
3 teaspoons vanilla
2¾ cups whole-wheat flour
1 teaspoon baking soda
3 teaspoons cinnamon
½ teaspoon baking powder
1 cup raisins

Preheat oven to 350°F.

In mixing bowl, combine egg substitute, oil, wheat germ, zucchini, bananas, and vanilla; mix at low speed of electric mixer until combined. In separate bowl, combine flour, baking soda, cinnamon, and baking powder. Gradually add flour mixture to zucchini mixture, blending well. Stir in raisins. Pour batter into two greased and floured loaf pans. Bake at 350°F for 1 hour.

NOTE: This quick bread is deliciously moist and very nutritious—an excellent example of a low-fat, low-cholesterol, low-sodium, and high-fiber food.

Makes 2 loaves.

*Nancy Gal, Ocala*
*Marion County Extension Home Economist*

# ❀ Corn Bread

2 cups self-rising cornmeal
¼ cup oil
1¼ cups milk
1 egg

Preheat oven and cast-iron skillet to 450°F.

In mixing bowl, combine cornmeal, oil, milk, and egg; mix well. Pour into preheated skillet. Bake at 450°F for 15-20 minutes.

*Tracy Jennings, Dade City*

## Sausage Spoon Bread

1 pound sausage links
4 cups milk
1 cup yellow cornmeal
2 tablespoons butter
½ teaspoon salt
2 tablespoons chopped onion
1 tablespoon prepared mustard
½ cup grated cheddar cheese
4 eggs, well beaten

In frying pan, brown sausage links on all sides; set aside to drain on paper toweling. Heat milk in top of double boiler; gradually stir in cornmeal. Cook cornmeal, stirring often, until mixture is the consistency of mush. Add butter and salt to cornmeal mixture; mix well. In mixing bowl, combine onion, mustard, cheese, and eggs; mix well. Gradually stir cornmeal mixture into egg mixture. Pour batter into greased 1½-quart baking dish; top with sausage. Bake at 425°F for 45 minutes.

Serves 6.

*National Pork Producers Council*

## Sausage Bread

2 pounds sausage
3 loaves frozen Bridgeford bread dough,
 thawed
6 eggs
1½ cups grated white cheese
1½ cups grated yellow cheese

In skillet, brown sausage; drain. Roll out thawed bread dough; cut into three equal pieces. Mix sausage with eggs and cheeses; divide mixture into three equal portions. Spread one portion of sausage mixture evenly over half of each piece of dough. Fold dough over and seal edges; place bread on greased baking sheet. Bake at 350°F for 20-25 minutes or until bread is golden brown.

Makes 3 loaves.

*Fannie L. Limoges, Tampa*

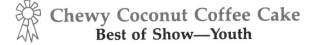 ## Chewy Coconut Coffee Cake
### Best of Show—Youth

¾ cup (1½ sticks) butter
2 cups sugar
6 eggs
1 (12-ounce) box vanilla wafers,
 crushed
1 (7-ounce) package coconut
½ cup milk
1 cup pecans, chopped

In mixing bowl, combine butter and sugar; cream together. Add eggs; beat well. Fold in vanilla wafer crumbs, coconut, milk, and nuts. Pour batter into greased and floured ten-inch tube pan. Bake at 325°F for 1 hour 15 minutes. Place pan on cooling rack and cool for 10 minutes. Remove cake from pan and cool completely on cooling rack.

*Kathy Parker, Hernando*

# German Coffee Cake

1 teaspoon baking soda
½ pint (1 cup) dairy sour cream
¼ pound (1 stick) butter
1 cup sugar
1 (3-ounce) package cream cheese,
  softened
2 eggs
2 cups cake flour
1½ teaspoons baking powder
1 teaspoon vanilla
½ cup chopped nuts
1 teaspoon cinnamon
½ cup sugar

Have all ingredients at room temperature.

In small bowl, combine soda and sour cream; set aside. In mixing bowl, cream butter and sugar. Add cream cheese, then add eggs; cream well. Combine flour and baking powder; sift together. Add dry ingredients to creamed mixture alternately with sour cream. Add vanilla; mix well. In small bowl, mix together nuts, cinnamon, and sugar. Pour one-third of the batter into a greased angel food cake pan or tube pan; sprinkle two-thirds of the nut mixture over batter in pan. Add remaining batter, then sprinkle with remaining nut mixture. Bake at 350°F for 45 minutes. Cool before removing from pan.

*Janet Kern, Tampa*

# Buttermilk Biscuits

3 cups sifted all-purpose flour
½ teaspoon baking soda
4 teaspoons baking powder
1 teaspoon salt
½ cup shortening
1 cup buttermilk

In mixing bowl, combine flour, soda, baking powder, and salt. Cut in shortening with fork or pastry blender until mixture looks like coarse meal. Add buttermilk; stir just enough to hold dough together. Place dough on floured board; roll out to ½-inch thickness. Cut dough with biscuit cutter; place biscuits on greased baking sheet. Bake at 475°F for 10-12 minutes.

Makes 20-24 large biscuits.

*Louise Powell, Sun City Center*

# Mary Jane's Orange Muffins

1 cup sugar
½ cup (1 stick) unsalted butter
2 eggs
1 cup buttermilk
½ cup chopped pecans
½ cup currants
2 cups sifted flour
½ teaspoon salt
1 teaspoon baking soda
1 teaspoon grated orange zest (peel)
Juice of 1 orange
½ cup sugar

In mixing bowl, cream one cup sugar and butter. Add eggs; beat until fluffy. Mix in buttermilk, pecans, and currants. Combine flour, salt, soda, and orange peel; add to creamed mixture, blending well. Spoon batter into greased muffin tins. Bake at 350°F until browned, about 20-25 minutes. While muffins are still warm, brush muffin tops with orange juice and sprinkle with sugar.

*Mary Jane Martinez, Tampa*

# Pumpkin Apple Streusel Muffins

2½ cups all-purpose flour
2 cups sugar
1 tablespoon pumpkin pie spice
1 teaspoon baking soda
½ teaspoon salt
2 eggs, slightly beaten
1 (29-ounce) can solid-pack pumpkin
½ cup vegetable oil
2 cups peeled, finely chopped apples

**STREUSEL TOPPING**

2 tablespoons all-purpose flour
¼ cup sugar
½ teaspoon cinnamon
4 tablespoons butter

To make Streusel Topping: In small bowl, combine flour, sugar, and cinnamon; cut in butter until mixture is crumbly. Set aside.

To make Muffins: In large bowl, combine flour, sugar, spice, baking soda, and salt; set aside. In medium bowl, combine eggs, pumpkin, and oil. Add liquid ingredients to dry ingredients; stir just until moistened. Stir in apples. Spoon batter into greased or paper-lined muffin cups, filling three-quarters full. Sprinkle streusel topping over batter. Bake at 350°F for 35-40 minutes.

*Coletta Squires, Tampa*

# Blueberry Pancakes

*2 large eggs*
*1¾ cups milk*
*¼ cup vegetable oil*
*2 cups all-purpose flour*
*2 tablespoons sugar*
*4 teaspoons baking powder*
*½ teaspoon salt*
*1½ cups fresh blueberries*
*½ cup powdered sugar (optional)*
*Syrup*

Heat griddle to medium-high heat (400°F).

In large bowl, beat eggs; stir in milk and oil. Lightly spoon flour into measuring cup to measure. Combine flour, sugar, baking powder, and salt; add to egg mixture, stirring just until large lumps disappear. Fold in blueberries. Lightly grease heated griddle. Pour batter, about ¼ cup at a time, onto hot griddle. Cook until bubbles form and edges start to dry, then turn and cook the other side. Sprinkle pancakes with powdered sugar and serve with syrup.

Makes 16 pancakes.

NOTE: For thinner pancakes, use additional milk. To test griddle, sprinkle a few drops of water on hot surface. When heat is just right, drops will sizzle and bounce.

*Doyle Conner, Tallahassee*

# Yeast Breads

 ## Cinnamon Bread

½ cup (1 stick) plus 2 tablespoons
   margarine
1 tablespoon plus 1 teaspoon sugar
1 teaspoon salt
1 package fast-rise yeast
¾ cup warm water (110°F)
½ cup milk, warmed
3¼ cups all-purpose flour, sifted
Water
½ cup brown sugar
2 teaspoons cinnamon

Insert dough hooks into mixer. Melt margarine; stir in sugar and salt. Dissolve yeast in warm water. Combine yeast with margarine mixture, mixing well. Blend in milk. Add one cup flour to yeast mixture; mix at medium speed of mixer until thoroughly combined, about 1 minute. Gradually add 1¼ cups flour and continue to mix for 3 minutes, scraping bowl once. Gradually add remaining one cup flour, scraping sides of bowl as needed. Mix and knead dough with mixer for an additional 4-6 minutes. The dough will form a ball and will clean the sides and bottom of the bowl.

(Be sure to run mixer continuously for the full mixing and kneading time, which should be 8-10 minutes. During the last couple of minutes of mixing time, it may become necessary to hand-guide the bowl to allow the dough hooks to knead the mixture.)

Shape dough into a ball; place in greased bowl, turning once to grease top of dough. Cover and let rise until double in bulk, about 1½ hours. Punch dough down; fold sides to center and turn dough over. Allow to rise again until double in bulk, about 40 minutes. Punch dough down; fold and turn dough, forming a 14x10-inch rectangle. Brush dough with water. Combine brown sugar and cinnamon in bowl or shaker; sprinkle cinnamon mixture over dough. Roll dough into a loaf; seal seams and ends. Place loaf in greased bread pan. Cover and let rise until double in bulk, about 30 minutes. Bake at 350°F for 50 minutes.

Makes 1 loaf.

*Ruth B. Ford, Montverde*

# Jalapeño Cheese Loaf

1 package dry yeast
1 cup warm water (105°F-115°F)
1 egg, beaten
2 tablespoons butter
4 to 4½ cups all-purpose flour, divided
1 tablespoon sugar
¾ teaspoon salt
¼ teaspoon garlic salt
3 small fresh jalapeño peppers, seeded
   and chopped
1 cup shredded sharp cheddar cheese
1 (4-ounce) jar pimientos, drained and
   diced
¼ cup minced onion

In large bowl, dissolve yeast in warm water; let stand for 5 minutes. Add egg and butter to yeast mixture; mix until butter melts. In separate bowl, combine three cups flour, sugar, salt, and garlic salt. Gradually add flour mixture to yeast mixture, beating at medium speed of electric mixer until smooth. Beat in peppers, cheese, pimientos, onion, and enough of the remaining flour to form a soft dough.

Turn out dough onto a well-floured surface; knead for 5-10 minutes or until smooth and elastic. Place dough in greased bowl, turning to grease top. Cover and let rise in a warm (85°F), draftfree place for 1 hour or until double in bulk. Punch dough down. Turn out dough onto a well-floured surface; knead for 1 minute. Shape dough into a loaf; place in greased 9x5x3-inch loaf pan. Cover and let rise in a warm place for 30 minutes or until double in bulk. Bake at 400°F for 40-45 minutes or until loaf sounds hollow when tapped. Remove from pan and cool on wire rack.

Makes 1 loaf.

NOTE: This recipe won Best of Show—Culinary honors at the Southwest Florida Fair.

*Pat Hunter, LaBelle*

# Onion Bread

3 to 3½ cups all-purpose flour
1 package fast-rise dry yeast
¼ cup instant dry milk powder
2 teaspoons granulated sugar
¾ teaspoon salt
3 tablespoons instant dry onions
¾ cup water
3 tablespoons corn oil
1 egg beaten with 1 tablespoon water
    (for brushing top of loaf)

In food processor fitted with a steel blade, combine one cup flour, yeast, milk powder, sugar, salt, and 2½ tablespoons dry onions (reserve remaining onions for garnishing loaf). Pulse processor on/off for 5 seconds to mix. In small saucepan, combine water and oil; heat to 125°F-130°F. With processor running, quickly add hot liquid through feed tube; process for 6-8 seconds. Add 1½ cups flour; process again for 6-8 seconds or until dough masses around blade and cleans the bowl. Dough will be stiff. Let dough stand in closed processor for 5 minutes. Meanwhile, lightly grease a small (8x4-inch) bread pan.

Turn out dough onto a lightly floured surface. Knead briefly, working in as much more flour as is needed to yield a smooth, elastic, fairly stiff dough. Shape dough into a smooth loaf, then transfer to greased bread pan. Brush top of loaf with egg-water mixture (reserve remaining mixture to brush again during baking). Set loaf aside, uncovered, in a very warm spot (80°F-90°F) for 25 minutes. Preheat oven to 400°F.

Using a sharp knife, make two or three ¼-inch cuts across the top of the loaf. Bake loaf at 400°F for 20 minutes. Remove from oven and brush both sides of slashes with egg-water mixture. Lightly sprinkle top with reserved dry onions. Return loaf to oven and continue baking for 8-12 additional minutes or until loaf is lightly browned and sounds hollow when tapped on the bottom. Transfer loaf to wire rack to cool. Serve warm or at room temperature with butter, or use for sandwiches.

Makes 1 medium-sized loaf.

*Ruth B. Ford, Montverde*

■ 89

 **Sourdough Bread**

*6 cups bread flour*
*2 teaspoons salt*
*⅓ cup sugar*
*1 cup sourdough starter, at room*
  *temperature*
*1⅓ cups warm water (105°F/40°C to*
  *115°F/45°C)*
*½ cup corn oil*
*Butter*

**SOURDOUGH STARTER**

*1 package active dry yeast*
*2½ cups warm water*
*1 cup flour*
*2 cups instant potatoes*
*1 teaspoon salt*
*½ cup sugar*

Prepare Sourdough Starter at least six days before making bread.

To make Sourdough Starter: In large bowl, dissolve yeast in warm water. Stir in flour, instant potatoes, salt, and sugar; beat until smooth. Place mixture in a two-quart glass container. Let stand, uncovered, at room temperature for three days, stirring mixture down several times a day. Cover container at night. Starter will increase in size as it begins to bubble and "work," and it will have a strong, yeasty smell. Cover and refrigerate after three to five days, transferring starter to a smaller container, if desired. (Makes about 2 cups starter.)

To make Bread: In large bowl (at least four-quart), combine flour, salt, and sugar. Make a well in center of dry ingredients and add starter, warm water, and ½ cup oil; beat until well blended. Oil top of dough, then cover with plastic wrap and let rise in a warm spot until tripled in size, 4-12 hours.

Generously grease three 8x4-inch or 8½x4½-inch loaf pans. Punch dough down. Turn out dough onto a floured surface and knead eight to ten times. Divide dough into three portions; shape each portion into a loaf. Place loaves in greased pans and set aside in a warm spot until tripled in bulk, 5-6 hours. (The small loaves may not fill pans—bread will rise another inch in the oven.)

Preheat oven to 350°F. Bake loaves for 30-40 minutes or until golden brown. Remove from oven; brush tops of loaves with butter. Remove from pans and place on wire rack to cool. Freeze for longer storage.

Makes 3 loaves.

*Ruth B. Ford, Montverde*

# Turtle Bread

2½ cups flour
1 package Quick-Rise yeast
1 tablespoon sugar
½ cup water
⅓ cup milk
1 tablespoon margarine
1 egg
2 raisins

In large bowl, combine 1½ cups flour, yeast, and sugar; mix well. In saucepan, combine water, milk, and margarine; heat to 125°F-130°F. Stir hot liquid into flour mixture. Stir in egg, then stir in enough remaining flour to make dough easy to handle. Sprinkle kneading surface with flour. Turn dough onto floured surface and knead until smooth and elastic, about 5 minutes. Cover dough and let rest for 10 minutes.

Lightly grease a cookie sheet. Shape a two-inch piece of dough into a ball to form the turtle's "head." Shape five one-inch pieces of dough into four "feet" and one "tail." Shape the remaining dough into a ball to form the turtle's "body." Place ball on greased cookie sheet and flatten slightly. Arrange head, feet, and tail around body, placing one end of each piece under the edge of the body to secure. Press raisins into head for eyes. Cover and let rise for 20 minutes.

Preheat oven to 400°F. Make crisscross cuts in body ¼ inch deep. Bake for 20-25 minutes.

*Nanci Wilhite, Polk City*

# Yeast Bread

4 cups flour
⅓ cup sugar
1 teaspoon salt
3 tablespoons shortening
2 packages dry yeast
1 cup warm water
2 tablespoons dry milk powder
1 egg, beaten

In large mixing bowl, combine flour, sugar, and salt; cut in shortening. In small bowl, dissolve yeast in warm water. Stir dry milk powder into yeast, then add to flour mixture along with egg. Knead dough until smooth, then let rise until double in bulk, about 45 minutes to 1 hour. Form dough into desired shapes. Place loaves in greased loaf pans, rolls on greased baking sheets. Bake at 350°F for 30 minutes.

*Joyce Downs, Brandon*

 # Crescent Dinner Rolls

½ cup milk
½ cup sugar
1½ teaspoons salt
¼ cup (½ stick) margarine
2 packages yeast
½ cup warm water
2 eggs, beaten
4½ cups (approximately) flour
2 tablespoons margarine, melted

Scald milk; stir in sugar, salt and margarine, then cool. In large bowl, dissolve yeast in warm water. Stir in milk mixture, eggs, and half of the flour; beat until smooth. Add remaining flour to make a slightly stiff dough. Knead dough on floured board until smooth, about 8 minutes. Place dough in greased bowl; cover and let rise for about 1 hour. Punch dough down; divide into two equal portions. Roll one portion into a large circle; brush with melted margarine. Cut circle into triangles, then roll up each triangle. Place rolls, tip down, on greased baking sheet. Repeat with the other portion of dough. Cover rolls and let rise for about 30 minutes. Bake at 400°F for approximately 10 minutes.

*June A. Moore, Tampa*

# Traditional English Muffins in a Loaf
## (Microwave Recipe)

5 cups unsifted flour
2 packages active dry yeast
1 tablespoon sugar
1 teaspoon salt
¼ teaspoon baking soda
1 cup dry milk powder
2½ cups water
Cornmeal

In large mixing bowl, combine three cups flour, undissolved yeast, sugar, salt, and soda. In saucepan, combine milk powder and water; heat until very warm (120°F-130°F). Add hot milk to dry ingredients; beat well. Stir in remaining flour to make a stiff batter. Spoon into two 8½x4½x2½-inch glass loaf pans that have been greased and sprinkled with cornmeal. Lightly sprinkle tops of loaves with cornmeal. Cover and let rise in a warm, draftfree place for 45 minutes. Microwave each loaf on high for 6½ minutes. Allow to rest for 5 minutes, then remove from pans. Cool. To serve, slice and toast.

Makes 2 loaves.

*Helen P. Webb, Seffner*
*Registered Dietitian*

# Refrigerator Biscuit

1 package yeast
1 cup warm water (110°F)
½ cup sugar
¾ cup oil
2 cups water
1 teaspoon salt
6 to 9 cups flour (enough to make a
    stiff dough)

Soften yeast in one cup warm water. In large mixing bowl, combine sugar, oil, two cups water, and salt; stir well. Add yeast mixture; mix well. Gradually add flour, one cup at a time, using enough flour to make a stiff dough. Turn out dough onto a floured board; knead until smooth, about 8-10 minutes. Shape dough into a ball; place in a large bowl that has been lightly greased, turning dough in bowl until entire surface is lightly greased. Cover bowl with plastic wrap; refrigerate overnight (24 hours). Dough will rise in the refrigerator to double its size.

To make biscuits, tear off a small amount of dough (about the size of a walnut) and roll into a ball; place on greased baking sheet and press down. Repeat with remaining dough. (Return any leftover dough to refrigerator to rise again or until you need it. Dough will keep up to a week in refrigerator.) Place baking sheet in warm place and let biscuits rise for about 3 hours. Bake at 400°F-450°F for 7-10 minutes.

*Rosanne Miller, Lutz*

## Maple Nut Coffee Cake
### Best of Show—Adult

¼ cup shortening
3 cups flour
2 packages yeast
¾ cup warm water
¼ cup sugar
2 teaspoons maple extract, divided
1 egg, beaten
½ cup sugar
⅓ cup chopped nuts
6 tablespoons butter, melted

**GLAZE**

1½ cups powdered sugar
¼ teaspoon maple extract
2 tablespoons milk
Chopped nuts

Grease a twelve-inch pizza pan; set aside.

In large bowl, cut shortening into flour. Dissolve yeast in warm water; add to flour mixture. Stir in ¼ cup sugar, 1 teaspoon maple extract, and egg; blend well. Cover and let rise in warm place until double in size, about 45 minutes to 1 hour. In small bowl, mix together ½ cup sugar, nuts, and 1 teaspoon maple extract. Press dough into greased pan. Brush with butter, then sprinkle with nut mixture. Cut into strips and twist. Cover and let rise for 30-40 minutes. Bake at 375°F for 30 minutes. Drizzle glaze over hot rolls. Sprinkle tops with chopped nuts.

To make Glaze: Combine powdered sugar, maple extract, and milk; beat until smooth.

*Joyce Downs, Brandon*

# DESSERTS

# Banana Ambrosia

6 large bananas (just ripe to underripe)
½ cup orange juice
1 orange, peeled, seeded and diced
1½ to 2 tablespoons dark brown sugar,
    firmly packed
½ cup shredded coconut or ¼ cup
    maraschino cherries (optional)

Spray a nine-inch pie plate with nonstick cooking spray. Peel bananas; cut in half crosswise, then cut into quarters lengthwise. Dip each piece of banana in orange juice, then arrange banana pieces in pie plate. In small bowl, combine remaining orange juice, diced orange, and brown sugar; mix until well blended. Spoon orange juice mixture over bananas. Bake at 350°F for 5-7 minutes or until bananas are soft and glazed. Just before serving, sprinkle with coconut or maraschino cherries. Serve hot or cold.

Serves 5.

*Helen P. Webb, Seffner*
*Registered Dietitian*

# Blueberry-Peach Streusel Cobbler

2 cups fresh blueberries
4 cups fresh peach slices (peeled)
½ cup sugar
¼ cup all-purpose flour
2 tablespoons lime juice

**STREUSEL TOPPING**

3¼ cups all-purpose flour
1 cup (2 sticks) butter, softened
¼ cup sugar
¼ cup light brown sugar, packed
1 teaspoon vanilla extract
1 teaspoon ground cinnamon
½ teaspoon salt

In 12x8-inch baking dish, combine blueberries, peaches, sugar, flour, and lime juice; mix thoroughly. Crumble Streusel Topping evenly over fruit mixture. Bake at 375°F for 45 minutes or until topping is golden. Serve warm or cool.

To prepare Streusel Topping: In large bowl, combine all topping ingredients; mix and knead with hands until smooth.

Serves 8.

*Florida Department of Agriculture and Consumer Services*

# Blueberry Bread Pudding

*2 tablespoons butter*
*4 large eggs, beaten*
*2½ cups milk*
*¾ cup sugar*
*2 tablespoons lime juice*
*8 cups French bread cubes (½-inch cubes)*
*2 cups fresh blueberries*

**CUSTARD SAUCE**

*2 large eggs*
*2 tablespoons sugar*
*1 cup milk, scalded*
*½ teaspoon vanilla extract*

Melt butter in 13x9x2-inch baking dish; set aside. In large bowl, combine eggs, milk, sugar, and lime juice; beat well. Add bread cubes, then let stand for 5 minutes. Fold in blueberries. Spoon mixture into prepared baking dish. Bake at 350°F for 35 minutes or until lightly browned and puffed. Serve warm with Custard Sauce.

To make Custard Sauce: In top of double boiler, combine eggs and sugar; beat well. Gradually stir ½ cup milk into egg mixture; add remaining milk, stirring constantly. Bring water in bottom of double boiler to a boil. Reduce heat to low; cook custard over hot water, stirring occasionally, for about 15 minutes or until mixture thickens. Cool slightly, then stir in vanilla. (Makes 1⅓ cups sauce.)

Serves 10.

*Florida Department of Agriculture and Consumer Services*

# Mango Fruit Deluxe

*2 mangos, sliced*
*1 cup mandarin orange sections, drained*
*1 cup pineapple chunks, drained*
*¼ cup maraschino cherries, halved*
*1 cup flaked coconut*
*1 cup miniature marshmallows*
*1 cup dairy sour cream*

Combine fruits with coconut and marshmallows, then fold sour cream into mixture. Cover and refrigerate several hours or overnight.

Serves 6-8.

*Florida Department of Agriculture and Consumer Services*

# Orange-Chocolate Mousse

6 (1-ounce) squares semisweet
  chocolate
1 teaspoon grated orange rind
¼ cup dark brown sugar
4 eggs
1 tablespoon orange juice
1½ cups heavy cream, whipped
Mandarin orange slices, for garnish
  (optional)

In top of double boiler, melt chocolate over hot water; cool. Combine orange rind, brown sugar, and eggs in blender container; blend until light and foamy. Add melted chocolate and orange juice; blend well. Fold in one cup whipped cream. Pour mixture into individual serving dishes; chill until set. Garnish each dish with a dollop of whipped cream and mandarin orange slices.

Serves 6.

NOTE: For a sweeter taste, use German sweet chocolate instead of semisweet chocolate.

*Florida Department of Agriculture and Consumer Services*

## Pecan Torte
### (Microwave Recipe)

14 graham crackers
1 cup sugar
1 teaspoon baking powder
½ teaspoon salt
3 eggs, separated
1 teaspoon vanilla
¾ cup chopped pecans
Chopped pecans (for garnish)
Whipped cream

Crush graham crackers; mix crumbs with sugar, baking powder, and salt. Lightly beat egg yolks; stir into dry ingredients. Beat egg whites until stiff, then fold into crumb mixture. Mix in vanilla and chopped pecans. Microwave at 70% power for 8-10 minutes. Remove from oven and let stand for 5 minutes before serving. Garnish with chopped pecans and serve with whipped cream.

Serves 8.

*Florida Department of Agriculture and Consumer Services*

# Strawberries Chantilly

2 cups whole strawberries (if extra-large, cut in half)
½ cup heavy cream
2 teaspoons confectioners' sugar
2 teaspoons light rum
2 tablespoons sweet cooking chocolate, grated

Hull berries, then place in sherbet glasses. In mixing bowl, combine cream, confectioners' sugar, and rum; whip with electric mixer until foamy and slightly thickened. Fold in grated chocolate. Spoon cream over strawberries.

Serves 3.

*Florida Department of Agriculture and Consumer Services*

# Baklava

1 pound walnuts or blanched almonds, chopped
½ cup sugar
½ teaspoon cinnamon
⅛ teaspoon ground cloves
1 pound sweet butter, melted
1 box Athens thin filo (strudel dough)

**SYRUP**

2 cups sugar
1 cup Tupelo honey
2 cups water
1 teaspoon lemon juice

Preheat oven to 375°F.

To prepare Syrup: In saucepan, combine all syrup ingredients. Bring to boil, then reduce heat and simmer for 10 minutes. Set aside to cool.

To assemble Baklava: In mixing bowl, combine walnuts, sugar, cinnamon, and cloves; set aside. Brush 12x17-inch baking tray with melted butter. Place eight filo leaves on buttered baking tray, brushing each leaf with melted butter. Spread half of the walnut mixture over filo leaves. Place seven of the remaining filo leaves over walnut mixture, brushing each leaf with melted butter. Spread remaining walnut mixture over filo leaves. Place last filo leaves on top of walnut mixture, brushing each with remaining butter. With a sharp knife, score the top filo leaves in diamond or square shapes in the sizes you desire. Bake at 375°F for 1 hour or until golden brown. Cool, then pour warm syrup evenly over baklava. Serve when cool.

*Ann Singletary, Tampa*

# Maple Meringue Grapefruit Cups

*2 grapefruit*
*½ cup reduced-calorie maple-flavored*
*  syrup, divided*
*3 egg whites, at room temperature*
*¼ teaspoon cream of tartar*

Preheat oven to 350°F.

Cut grapefruit in half. Loosen and remove grapefruit sections; set aside. Scoop out membrane from shells and discard. Place grapefruit shells in shallow baking pan. In small bowl, toss together reserved grapefruit sections and ¼ cup syrup; divide mixture evenly among grapefruit shells. Bake at 350°F for 5-10 minutes or until heated through.

In small bowl, beat egg whites at high speed of electric mixer until foamy. Add cream of tartar; gradually beat in remaining ¼ cup syrup until stiff peaks form. Spoon meringue evenly onto grapefruit in shells. Bake at 350°F for 10-15 minutes longer or until meringue is set and golden brown.

Serves 4.

*Florida Department of Citrus*

# CAKES

## Fresh Apple Cake
### Best of Show—Adult

3 cups peeled and chopped raw apples
1½ cups vegetable oil
2½ cups sugar
3 eggs
2½ cups flour, sifted
¼ teaspoon baking soda
1 teaspoon salt
3 teaspoons pumpkin pie spice
1 teaspoon cinnamon
1 tablespoon vanilla
1 cup chopped pecans

Prepare apples; set aside. In large bowl, combine oil, sugar and eggs; beat well. Combine flour, baking soda, salt, pumpkin pie spice, and cinnamon; sift together, then add gradually to creamed mixture. Mix in vanilla; gently fold in apples and pecans. Pour batter into greased and floured 13x9-inch cake pan. Bake at 350°F for 1 hour.

*Coletta Squires, Tampa*

## Carrot Cake

2 cups sugar
4 eggs
1½ cups corn oil
2 cups cake flour, sifted
2 teaspoons baking powder
2 teaspoons baking soda
2 teaspoons cinnamon
1 teaspoon salt
2 teaspoons vanilla
3 cups finely grated carrots
1 cup finely chopped black walnuts
Nut meats (for decoration, if desired)

**RUM BUTTERCREAM FROSTING**

1 (1-pound) box confectioners' sugar
1 cup (2 sticks) sweet butter
1 to 1½ teaspoons white rum extract
2 to 3 tablespoons hot milk

Measure sugar into mixing bowl; add eggs, one at a time, beating until fluffy. Add oil; mix well. Combine flour, baking powder, baking soda, cinnamon, and salt; add to creamed mixture and blend well. Add vanilla, carrots, and walnuts; blend well. Grease three eight-inch round cake pans, flour lightly, and line with waxed paper. Pour batter into prepared pans. Bake at 350°F for 30-40 minutes or until a toothpick inserted in center of cake comes out clean. Cool for 5 minutes in pans, then remove from pans and cool completely before frosting with Rum Buttercream Frosting. Decorate frosted cake with nut meats, if desired.

To make Rum Buttercream Frosting: In mixing bowl, combine confectioners' sugar, butter, and rum extract; beat well. Gradually beat in milk.

*Ruth B. Ford, Montverde*

# Carrot Cake

2 cups all-purpose flour
2 teaspoons baking soda
2 teaspoons cinnamon
2 cups sugar
1½ cups Wesson or Crisco oil
4 large eggs
3 cups grated carrots

## ICING

1 (1-pound) box confectioners' sugar
1 (8-ounce) package cream cheese
½ cup (1 stick) margarine, softened
2 teaspoons vanilla
1 cup finely chopped pecans

Combine flour, soda, and cinnamon; sift together, then set aside. In mixing bowl, beat sugar into oil; add eggs one at a time, beating well. Stir in dry ingredients. Add grated carrots; mix well. Pour batter into four greased and floured nine-inch cake pans. Bake at 350°F for 25-30 minutes. Cool. Frost cooled cake with icing.

To make Icing: In mixing bowl, combine confectioners' sugar, cream cheese, and margarine; cream together. Stir in vanilla and chopped nuts; blend well. Frost cooled cake layers with icing.

Serves 18-20.

NOTE: I grate my carrots on the coarse side of a hand grater. Be sure to grate, not shred.

*Willie H. Haas, McAlpin*

# Chocolate Pound Cake
## (Filled)

¾ cup (1½ sticks) butter
2 cups sugar
1 teaspoon vanilla
4 eggs
2 cups flour
¼ cup cocoa
1 teaspoon baking powder
¼ teaspoon salt
1 cup dairy sour cream

**FILLING**

1 cup miniature chocolate chips
½ cup chopped pecans
1/3 cup sweetened condensed milk

**GLAZE**

1 cup powdered sugar
2 tablespoons cocoa
2 tablespoons butter, softened
2 to 3 tablespoons milk

To make Filling: In mixing bowl, combine chocolate chips, pecans, and sweetened condensed milk. Mix together well; set aside.

To make Cake: In mixing bowl, combine butter and sugar; cream together. Add vanilla and eggs; beat for 3 minutes. Combine flour, cocoa, baking powder, and salt. Add dry ingredients to creamed mixture alternately with sour cream; beat for 3 minutes. Pour half of the cake batter into greased and floured twelve-cup bundt pan. Spoon filling around center of batter, then add remaining cake batter. Bake at 350°F for 60-65 minutes. Cool in pan for 45 minutes (do not invert pan), then turn out onto cake plate and continue cooling. Drizzle glaze over cooled cake.

To make Glaze: In mixing bowl, combine powdered sugar, cocoa, butter, and milk; beat until smooth.

*Doris Swank, Naples*

# Chocolate Angel Food Cake

*1 cup minus 2 tablespoons cake flour*
*2 tablespoons cocoa*
*¾ cup sugar*
*12 egg whites*
*1½ teaspoons cream of tartar*
*¼ teaspoon salt*
*1 teaspoon vanilla*
*¾ cup sugar*

## ICING

*½ cup (1 stick) butter*
*¼ cup cocoa*
*3½ cups confectioners' sugar*
*4 to 5 tablespoons milk*

Combine cake flour, cocoa, and ¾ cup sugar; sift together, then set aside. In mixing bowl, combine egg whites, cream of tartar, salt, and vanilla; beat until soft peaks form. Continue beating and add ¾ cup sugar, one tablespoon at a time, until stiff peaks form. Sprinkle dry ingredients on top of egg whites, one-fourth at a time, and fold in. Pour batter into ungreased ten-inch tube pan. Gently cut through batter with a spatula to break bubbles. Bake at 375°F for 40 minutes. To cool, invert pan on funnel. Cool cake completely before removing from pan. Spread icing over cooled cake.

To make Icing: In mixing bowl, combine all ingredients; beat until desired consistency is obtained.

*Doris Swank, Naples*

# Deep Dark Chocolate Cake

1¾ cups all-purpose flour
¾ cup cocoa
2 cups sugar
1½ teaspoons baking soda
1½ teaspoons baking powder
1 teaspoon salt
2 eggs
1 cup milk
½ cup vegetable oil
2 teaspoons vanilla
1 cup boiling water

**DARK CHOCOLATE
BUTTERCREAM FROSTING**

6 tablespoons butter, softened
¾ cup cocoa
3⅔ cups confectioners' sugar
¼ cup milk
1 teaspoon vanilla

Preheat oven to 350°F. Grease and flour two 9x1½-inch round pans; set aside.

In large mixing bowl, combine flour, cocoa, sugar, baking soda, baking powder, and salt. Add eggs, milk, oil, and vanilla; beat for 2 minutes on medium speed of electric mixer. By hand, stir in boiling water (batter will be thin). Pour batter into prepared pans. Bake at 350°F for 30-35 minutes. Cool cakes for 10 minutes, then remove from pans. Cool completely on wire rack. Frost cooled cake with Dark Chocolate Buttercream Frosting.

To make Dark Chocolate Buttercream Frosting: In small mixing bowl, cream butter. Add cocoa and confectioners' sugar to butter alternately with milk; beat until desired spreading consistency is obtained (additional milk may be needed). Blend in vanilla. (Makes about 2 cups frosting.)

*Helen M. Campbell, Valrico*

# German Chocolate Sour Cream Cake

4 ounces sweet baking chocolate
½ cup hot water
1 cup (2 sticks) butter
2 cups sugar
4 eggs, separated
1 teaspoon vanilla
2½ cups cake flour
1 teaspoon baking soda
½ teaspoon salt
1 cup dairy sour cream

## FROSTING

1 cup evaporated milk
1 cup sugar
3 egg yolks, unbeaten
1 cup (2 sticks) butter
1 teaspoon vanilla
1⅓ cups coconut
1 cup chopped pecans

Melt chocolate in hot water; set aside to cool. In mixing bowl, cream butter and sugar until light and fluffy. Add egg yolks, one at a time, to creamed mixture, beating after each addition. Add vanilla and cooled chocolate; mix well. Combine cake flour, baking soda, and salt; sift together. Add dry ingredients to creamed mixture alternately with sour cream, beating well after each addition. Beat egg whites until stiff, then fold into batter. Pour batter into three greased and floured nine-inch cake pans. Bake at 350°F for 25-30 minutes. Cool for 10 minutes, then turn out of pans to continue cooling. Frost tops of layers only.

To make Frosting: In saucepan, combine evaporated milk, sugar, egg yolks, and butter. Cook over medium heat for 12-15 minutes or until thickened, stirring constantly. Add vanilla, coconut, and pecans. Beat until cool.

*Doris Swank, Naples*

*A favorite*
*In the box*

# Texas Chocolate Cake

2 cups all-purpose flour
2 cups sugar
½ cup (1 stick) margarine
½ cup shortening
6 tablespoons cocoa
1 cup water
2 eggs, well beaten
½ cup buttermilk
1 teaspoon baking soda
1 teaspoon vanilla

## ICING

½ cup (1 stick) margarine
4 tablespoons cocoa
6 tablespoons cream
1 (16-ounce) box confectioners' sugar
1 teaspoon vanilla
1 cup coconut

Preheat oven to 400°F.

In large bowl, sift together flour and sugar. In saucepan, combine margarine, shortening, cocoa, and water; bring to boil. Pour cocoa mixture over flour mixture; beat together. In another bowl, combine eggs, buttermilk, soda, and vanilla. Add to creamed mixture; blend well. Pour batter into greased and floured 13x9x2-inch pan. Bake at 400°F for 30 minutes. Spread icing over hot cake as soon as you remove it from the oven.

To make Icing: In saucepan, combine margarine, cocoa, and cream; bring to boil. Remove from heat. Add confectioners' sugar, vanilla, and coconut to hot mixture; mix well.

NOTE: Do not wash saucepan between cake and icing—just reuse. This is a delicious, moist cake—so easy to make, carry, and serve. Clean kitchen to clean kitchen in less than 1 hour.

*Paula P. Stanley, Inverness*

# Coconut-Pineapple Cake

1 cup (2 sticks) butter, melted
2 cups sugar
4 eggs
3 cups Soft-as-Silk cake flour
2½ teaspoons baking powder
1 cup milk

## FILLING

2 cups sugar
1 (8-ounce) carton dairy sour cream
2 (8-ounce) packages frozen coconut,
   thawed
1 cup crushed pineapple, drained

To make Filling: In top of double boiler, combine sugar, sour cream, coconut, and pineapple; mix well. Cook over hot water (so mixture does not burn on the bottom) until thickened, stirring frequently. Set aside to cool.

To make Cake: In mixing bowl, cream butter and sugar. Add eggs, one at a time, blending well after each addition. Combine flour and baking powder; sift together. Add dry ingredients to creamed mixture alternately with milk; beat for 4 minutes. Grease and lightly flour three layer cake pans. Pour batter into prepared cake pans. Bake at 350°F for 25-35 minutes or until a toothpick inserted in center of cake comes out clean. Cool slightly, then remove from pans and cool completely before spreading with filling.

NOTE: Make filling before mixing cake so sugar will have time to melt, and so filling can cool while you are preparing cake. If you do not want to use pineapple in the filling, omit pineapple and use three packages of coconut instead. This is a rich cake, but it is something special and different.

*Ruth B. Ford, Montverde*

# Company Scratch Cake

2½ cups self-rising flour
⅔ cup solid shortening
1⅔ cups sugar
1¼ cups milk, divided
3 eggs
1 teaspoon vanilla extract

**FROSTING**

1 (8-ounce) package cream cheese, at
  room temperature
2 cups confectioners' sugar, packed like
  brown sugar
1 tablespoon vanilla extract
1 tablespoon (more or less) milk
1 (8-ounce) container Cool Whip,
  thawed

**FRUIT TOPPING**

1 (8-ounce) package frozen sweetened
  strawberries, thawed
1 tablespoon cornstarch

In mixing bowl, combine flour, shortening, sugar, and ¾ cup milk; beat for 2 minutes with electric mixer. Add remaining milk, eggs, and vanilla extract; beat for another 2 minutes. Pour batter into two well-greased and floured nine-inch cake pans. Bake at 350°F until center springs back when touched with finger, about 30-35 minutes. Cool. Spread frosting over cooled cake layers, making a slight indentation in frosting on top of cake. Fill indentation with chilled Fruit Topping.

To make Frosting: In mixing bowl, combine cream cheese, confectioners' sugar, vanilla extract, and milk; mix until smooth. Add Cool Whip; mix well.

To make Fruit Topping: In small bowl, mix some juice from strawberries with cornstarch, stirring well to prevent lumping. In saucepan, combine cornstarch mixture with strawberries; cook until mixture is clear and slightly thickened. Cool, then refrigerate until cold.

Serves 12-16.

NOTE: Blueberries or cherries may be used in place of strawberries. Amount of milk used in frosting will vary depending on the humidity.

*Patricia S. Green, Raiford*

## Fruitcake

1½ cups mixed candied fruit
2 cups light raisins
2 cups dark raisins
1 cup currants
2 cups mincemeat
3 cups nuts (combination of walnuts,
    pecans, and black walnuts)
3½ cups all-purpose flour
1 cup sugar
1 teaspoon salt
2 eggs, beaten
¾ cup corn oil
2 teaspoons vanilla
1½ teaspoons baking soda
2 tablespoons boiling water

In mixing bowl, combine candied fruit, light and dark raisins, currants, mincemeat, and nuts; set aside. Combine flour, sugar, and salt; sift together. Combine fruit mixture with dry ingredients; mix well. In a separate bowl, beat eggs; add oil and vanilla. Combine egg mixture with fruit mixture; mix well. Dissolve soda in boiling water; stir into batter, mixing until well blended. Pour batter into a ten-inch tube pan lined with heavy brown paper that has been oiled. Bake at 275°F for 2½ hours. Let cake cool for 1 hour before removing from pan.

NOTE: You can decorate the cake with candied fruit (cherries, pineapple, etc.) and nut meats before baking, if desired.

*Ruth B. Ford, Montverde*

## Pecan Dump Cake

1 can crushed pineapple
1 cup light brown sugar
1 package yellow cake mix
1 cup chopped pecans
½ cup (1 stick) margarine, melted

Grease and flour a 9x12-inch pan. Empty pineapple into pan. Sprinkle brown sugar over pineapple. Spread dry cake mix over brown sugar. Sprinkle pecans over cake mix. Pour melted margarine over pecans. Bake at 325°F for approximately 50 minutes.

Serves 16.

*Paula P. Stanley, Inverness*

# Peanut Butter Cake

½ cup smooth peanut butter
⅓ cup butter
1½ cups granulated sugar
2 eggs, beaten
1 teaspoon vanilla
2 cups cake flour, sifted
1 tablespoon baking powder
1 teaspoon salt
½ teaspoon cinnamon
1 cup milk

## PEANUT-COCOA FROSTING

2 cups confectioners' sugar, sifted
⅓ cup cocoa
½ cup crunchy peanut butter
6 or 7 tablespoons milk
1 teaspoon vanilla

Preheat oven to 350°F.

In mixing bowl, combine peanut butter and butter; cream thoroughly. Gradually add sugar and continue beating until mixture is light and fluffy. Add eggs; stir in vanilla. Sift together flour, baking powder, salt, and cinnamon. Add dry ingredients to creamed mixture alternately with milk, beginning and ending with dry ingredients and beating well after each addition. Pour batter into greased and floured 9x13-inch cake pan. Bake at 350°F for 30 minutes or until cake tests done. Cool. Frost cooled cake with Peanut-Cocoa Frosting.

To make Peanut-Cocoa Frosting: Combine confectioners' sugar and cocoa; sift together into mixing bowl. Add peanut butter; cream well. Add milk and vanilla; continue beating until smooth.

*Florida Peanut Producers Association, Graceville*

# Poppy Seed Pound Cake with Rum Sauce

*1 pound (4 sticks) butter, softened*
*3 cups sugar*
*6 eggs*
*1 tablespoon grated orange rind*
*1½ teaspoons vanilla*
*½ cup milk*
*4 cups all-purpose flour*
*¼ cup orange juice*
*½ cup poppy seeds*

**RUM SAUCE**

*⅔ cup rum*
*1 cup confectioners' sugar*
*¼ teaspoon orange rind*
*¼ teaspoon vanilla*

In mixing bowl, cream butter. Add sugar; continue beating until light and fluffy. Add eggs, one at a time, beating well after each addition. Add grated orange rind. Combine vanilla and milk. Add flour to creamed mixture alternately with milk and orange juice. Add poppy seeds; mix well. Pour batter into greased and floured ten-inch tube pan. Bake at 300°F for 1½ to 1¾ hours or until done. Spoon Rum Sauce over cake. Wrap cake in plastic wrap for 8 hours.

To make Rum Sauce: Combine all ingredients; stir until well blended.

*Audrey Schroeder, Tampa*

# Cheesecake
## Best of Show—Young American

**CRUST**

*1 cup graham-cracker crumbs*
*½ cup sugar*
*½ cup vegetable oil*

**FILLING**

*8 eggs*
*2 cups sugar*
*2 cups dairy sour cream*
*5 (8-ounce) packages cream cheese, softened*
*3 tablespoons vanilla extract*

To make Crust: Combine graham-cracker crumbs, sugar, and vegetable oil; mix well. Place crumb mixture on bottom of a nine-inch springform pan; set aside.

To make Filling: In mixing bowl, combine eggs, sugar, sour cream, cream cheese, and vanilla; beat until well blended. Pour filling mixture over crust. Bake at 375°F for 50 minutes. Remove from oven. Refrigerate for 8 hours before serving.

*Jeffrey Hutchinson, Sarasota*

# Blueberry Cheesecake

**CRUST**

*1 cup crushed butter biscuit cookies*
*3 tablespoons butter, melted*

**FILLING**

*3 (8-ounce) packages cream cheese,*
  *softened*
*¾ cup sugar*
*3 large eggs*
*1 teaspoon vanilla extract*

**TOPPING**

*4 cups fresh blueberries*
*1 cup sugar*
*2 tablespoons cornstarch*
*1 teaspoon lime juice*
*1 tablespoon Grand Marnier liqueur*

To make Crust: In mixing bowl, combine cookie crumbs and butter; mix together. Press mixture into the bottom of an eight-inch springform pan to form crust; set aside.

To make Filling: In mixing bowl, combine cream cheese and sugar; mix at medium speed of electric mixer until well blended. Add eggs, one at a time, mixing well after each addition. Blend in vanilla. Pour filling mixture over crust. Bake at 450°F for 10 minutes, then reduce oven temperature to 325°F and continue baking for 45 minutes. Loosen cake from rim of pan to cool. Refrigerate until chilled.

To make Topping: In saucepan, mix together blueberries, sugar, cornstarch, lime juice, and liqueur. Cook over medium heat until mixture thickens. Cool, then spread over chilled cheesecake.

Serves 10-12.

*Florida Department of Agriculture and Consumer Services*

# Cheesecake Contentment

4 (8-ounce) packages cream cheese,
    softened
1½ cups sugar
5 eggs
1 pint (2 cups) dairy sour cream
2 tablespoons cornstarch
2 tablespoons lemon juice
1 teaspoon vanilla flavoring
½ cup (1 stick) butter, melted

In mixing bowl, combine cream cheese and sugar; beat until fluffy. Add eggs, one at a time, beating well after each addition. Add sour cream, cornstarch, lemon juice, and vanilla; mix well. Add butter; mix well. Pour mixture into well-greased springform pan. Place springform pan in a larger pan containing one inch of water. Bake at 350°F for 1 hour. Turn off heat and leave cake in oven for an additional 10 minutes. Cool cake completely before serving.

Serves 16.

NOTE: This is absolutely "the best" cheesecake. Does not need any fruit topping.

*Gloria Cuyler, Inverness*

# Chocolate Amaretto Cheesecake

## CRUST

15 graham crackers, crushed
1 tablespoon sugar
1 tablespoon butter, melted

## FILLING

3½ (8-ounce) packages cream cheese,
  softened
5 eggs
1 cup sugar
1 (12-ounce) package chocolate chips,
  melted
1½ teaspoons vanilla

## TOPPING

1 (16-ounce) container dairy sour cream
½ cup granulated sugar
1½ teaspoons vanilla
2 (1.53-ounce) Hershey bars, melted

To make Crust: Combine graham-cracker crumbs, sugar, and butter; mix well. Press mixture into bottom and sides of buttered pie plate to form crust; set aside.

To make Filling: In mixing bowl, beat cream cheese until light and fluffy. Add eggs, one at a time, beating well after each addition. Add sugar slowly, mixing well. Add melted chocolate chips and vanilla; beat until thoroughly combined. Pour filling into graham-cracker crust. Bake at 300°F for 1 hour.

To make Topping: While cake is baking, combine sour cream, sugar, vanilla, and melted Hershey bars in mixing bowl; mix well. Remove cake from oven after 1 hour. Spread topping over hot cake. Return cake to oven for 10 minutes, then turn off oven and leave cake in oven for 1 additional hour.

*Mrs. Lewie A. Hunter, Dunedin*

**Creamy Lime Cheesecake**
**Best of Show—Youth**

## CRUST

*15 chocolate graham crackers, crushed*
*1 teaspoon butter, melted*

## FILLING

*3 (8-ounce) packages Philadelphia*
*cream cheese, softened*
*5 eggs*
*1½ cups sugar*
*6 tablespoons fresh lime juice*
*2 teaspoons grated lime rind*

## TOPPING

*1 (16-ounce) carton dairy sour cream*
*2 tablespoons lime juice*
*½ cup granulated sugar*
*2 drops green food coloring*
*1 drop yellow food coloring*

To make Crust: Combine graham-cracker crumbs and butter; mix thoroughly. Press in bottom only of buttered pan; set aside.

To make Filling: In mixing bowl, beat cream cheese until light and fluffy. Add eggs, one at a time, beating well after each addition. Add sugar very slowly, then add lime juice and grated lime rind; mix well. Pour filling into crust. Bake at 300°F for 1 hour.

To make Topping: While cake is baking, combine sour cream, lime juice, sugar, and food colorings in mixing bowl; mix well. Remove cake from oven after 1 hour. Carefully spread topping over hot cake. Return cake to oven for 10 minutes. DO NOT OPEN OVEN DOOR AGAIN. Now turn off oven and leave cake in oven for 1 additional hour. This prevents the topping from cracking.

*Julie K. Hunter, Dunedin*

# Praline Ice Cream Cake

12 Vienna fingers (cookies)
½ gallon Tin Lizzy ice cream (vanilla ice cream with caramel swirls and chocolate-covered toffee tidbits)
1 small jar caramel sauce
1 small container Cool Whip, thawed
½ cup chopped pecans
1 (3-ounce) Nestlé milk chocolate bar, shaved

Crush Vienna fingers (with centers left in). Place cookie crumbs in the bottom of a ten-inch springform pan; freeze for 1 hour. Soften ice cream for a few minutes so it is easy to work with. Spoon softened ice cream on top of crushed cookies; freeze for 2 hours. Top ice cream with caramel sauce; freeze for 1 hour. Top caramel sauce with Cool Whip, chopped pecans, and shaved chocolate bar; freeze. Use hot knife to cut cake into serving pieces.

Serves 8-10.

NOTE: This is an original recipe, created by Janice.

Janice Tesar, Lake Mary

# PIES

# Apple Praline Pie

4 cups raw apple slices
1 tablespoon fresh lemon juice
2 tablespoons Minute Tapioca
¾ cup white sugar
½ teaspoon cinnamon
½ cup brown sugar
½ cup white flour
¼ cup (½ stick) butter or margarine
1 cup chopped walnuts
1 unbaked pie shell
Shredded coconut

In large bowl, combine apples, lemon juice, and tapioca. Add white sugar and cinnamon; stir together, then set aside. In mixing bowl, combine brown sugar, flour, and butter; mix together until crumbly. Add chopped nuts; mix well. Spoon half of the crumbly mixture onto the bottom of an unbaked pie shell. Stir apple mixture again, then spoon on top of crumbly mixture. Top with remaining crumbly mixture. Bake at 400°F for about 10 minutes, then reduce heat to 350°F and continue baking until apples are tender, about 45-50 minutes. Sprinkle top with shredded coconut and return pie to oven just until coconut is browned. Remove from oven and serve warm.

Serves 6.

NOTE: Super for kids, young and old, who love warm apple pie.

*Sandy Russell, Gainesville*

## French Coconut Pie
### Best of Show—Adult

1¼ cups sugar
1 tablespoon flour
¼ cup (½ stick) margarine, melted
3 eggs
1 teaspoon vanilla
¼ cup buttermilk
1 (3½-ounce) can coconut
1 unbaked pie shell

In this order, mix together sugar, flour, and margarine. Add eggs and vanilla, then add buttermilk and coconut; mix well. Pour filling into unbaked pie shell. Bake at 400°F for 10 minutes, then reduce heat to 300°F and bake for 45-50 minutes.

*Mrs. Lewie A. Hunter, Dunedin*

# Calamondin Pie

½ cup calamondin* puree
1½ cups boiling water
1 cup sugar
3 tablespoons flour
⅛ teaspoon salt
3 tablespoons cornstarch
2 eggs, separated
1 tablespoon butter
1 (9-inch) baked pie shell
Few grains of salt
4 tablespoons sugar (for meringue)

To prepare calamondin puree: Remove seeds from fruit but do not peel. Cut fruit into quarters; liquefy in blender. Set aside.

To make pie filling: In saucepan, combine boiling water, sugar, flour, salt, and cornstarch. Bring to boil over medium heat. Reduce heat to low, cover, and cook for 5-7 minutes. Whisk in beaten egg yolks; cook for 2 additional minutes, stirring constantly. Remove from heat. Blend in butter and calamondin puree. Cool slightly, then pour filling into baked pie shell.

To make meringue: Beat egg whites with a few grains of salt until soft peaks form. Add four tablespoons sugar gradually, beating until stiff. Spread meringue over top of pie. Bake at 400°F for 7 minutes.

Serves 6-8.

*NOTE: Calamondins are a beautiful Florida citrus fruit resembling a tiny sour orange.

*WRB Enterprises, Inc., Tampa*

# Kentucky Derby Pie
## Best of Show—Young American

2 eggs
½ cup flour
½ cup granulated sugar
½ cup brown sugar
1 cup (2 sticks) butter, melted
1 cup chocolate chips
1 cup chopped walnuts
1 unbaked pie shell

In large bowl, beat eggs until foamy. Add flour, granulated sugar, and brown sugar; beat until well blended. Blend in butter, then stir in chocolate chips and walnuts. Pour into unbaked pie shell. Bake at 325°F for 1 hour. Serve warm.

*Alice Seith, Homosassa*

# Lemon Meringue Pie

**PIE CRUST**

1½ cups flour
½ teaspoon salt
½ cup Crisco shortening
5 tablespoons cold water

**LEMON FILLING & MERINGUE**

3 tablespoons cornstarch
1¼ cups granulated sugar
¼ cup lemon juice
1 tablespoon grated lemon peel
3 eggs, separated
1½ cups boiling water
6 tablespoons granulated sugar

To make Pie Crust: In mixing bowl, combine flour and salt. Cut in shortening until mixture is crumbly. Add water; mix well. Form dough into two balls; roll out to make two crusts. Fit crusts into two pie plates; bake at 425°F for 8-10 minutes or until crusts are lightly browned. (Makes 2 single-crusts or 1 double-crust.)

To make Lemon Filling: In saucepan, combine cornstarch, 1¼ cups sugar, lemon juice, and lemon peel; mix well. In small mixing bowl, beat egg yolks; stir yolks into mixture in saucepan. Gradually stir in boiling water. Bring to boil, stirring constantly, and continue cooking until mixture thickens. Pour filling into baked pie shell.

To make Meringue: Beat egg whites until stiff, then gradually beat in six tablespoons sugar. Spread meringue over top of pie.

Bake pie at 425°F for 4-5 minutes.

*Gladys Painter, Brandon*

# Florida Key Lime Pie

1 cup sugar
¼ cup flour
3 tablespoons cornstarch
½ teaspoon salt
2 cups water
3 egg yolks, beaten
1 tablespoon butter
¼ cup Key lime juice
1 teaspoon (or more) grated lime peel
1 (9-inch) baked pie crust

In saucepan, combine sugar, flour, cornstarch, and salt; stir in water. Cook over medium heat, stirring until thick. Stir small amount of hot mixture into egg yolks, then stir egg yolks into mixture in pan. Cook for 2 minutes. Stir in butter, lime juice, and lime peel. Pour mixture into baked pie crust.

Serves 6-8.

*Martha Woeste, Gainesville*

# Key Lime Chiffon Pie

1 tablespoon unflavored gelatin
½ cup cold water
2 eggs, separated
1¼ cups sugar, divided
¼ teaspoon salt
½ cup Key lime juice, divided
2 drops yellow food coloring (optional)
1 (8-ounce) container whipped topping, thawed (reserve a small amount for top of pie)
Lime slices (for garnish; I use candied lime slices)
1 baked pie shell

In small bowl, soften gelatin in water. In top of double boiler, combine egg yolks, one cup sugar, salt, and ¼ cup lime juice; cook until mixture thickens. Pour mixture into medium-size bowl; add remaining lime juice and softened gelatin. Add food coloring at this time, if desired; mix thoroughly. Place mixture in freezer, stirring every 15 minutes, until thickened. Beat egg whites with remaining ¼ cup sugar, then fold thickened gelatin mixture into egg whites. Fold in whipped topping. Pile filling into baked pie shell. Garnish edge of pie with reserved topping and lime slices.

Serves 8.

NOTE: This recipe won first place at the 1981 Florida State Fair.

*Shirley J. Myrsiades, Clearwater*

# Muscadine Pie

4 cups Muscadine grapes
¾ cup sugar
1 teaspoon lemon juice
1 teaspoon quick-cooking tapioca
1 tablespoon grated orange rind
    (optional)
¼ teaspoon cinnamon (optional)
Pastry for 1 (9-inch) lattice-top pie
2 tablespoons margarine or butter,
    melted

Preheat oven to 450°F.

Seed grapes, reserving juice. In mixing bowl, combine grapes (including juice), sugar, lemon juice, tapioca, orange rind, and cinnamon; let mixture sit for 15 minutes. Pour mixture into unbaked pie shell, then cover with lattice top. Brush lattice top with margarine. Bake at 450°F for 10 minutes, then reduce heat to 350°F and bake for an additional 20 minutes. Cool. Serve plain, with whipped topping, or with vanilla ice cream.

*Florida Grape Growers Association, Tampa*

## Peanut Butter Pie
### Best of Show—Youth

1 (8-ounce) package cream cheese,
    softened
½ cup peanut butter
1 cup confectioners' sugar
½ cup milk
1 (8-ounce) container Cool Whip,
    thawed
1 graham-cracker pie crust

In mixing bowl, beat cream cheese until creamy. Add peanut butter and confectioners' sugar, then slowly add milk; mix well. Fold in Cool Whip; blend thoroughly. Pour filling into crust. Freeze for 4-6 hours. Remove from freezer 10 minutes before serving.

*J'aime Irish, Inverness*

# Peanut Butter Pie

1 (3-ounce) package cream cheese, softened
1 cup sugar
½ cup crunchy peanut butter
1 (8-ounce) container Cool Whip, thawed
1 graham-cracker pie crust or other baked pastry shell
¼ cup finely chopped peanuts

In mixing bowl, combine cream cheese and sugar; cream together well. Add peanut butter, then fold in Cool Whip, blending well. Pour mixture into prepared crust. Sprinkle top of pie with chopped peanuts. Refrigerate overnight or until well chilled.

Serves 8.

NOTE: Levy County grows lots of peanuts. We serve this pie at Peanut Short Course.

*Barbara Sapp, Williston*

 # Southern Pecan Pie

**FLAKY OIL PASTRY**

2 cups flour
1 teaspoon salt
½ cup vegetable oil
5 tablespoons cold water

**FILLING**

3 eggs
⅔ cup sugar
Dash of salt
1 cup light corn syrup
⅓ cup butter, melted
1 cup pecan halves

To make Flaky Oil Pastry: Combine flour and salt; sift into mixing bowl. Combine oil and water, but do not stir. Add oil mixture to dry ingredients; stir together with a fork. Form dough into two balls. Roll out one ball between two sheets of waxed paper. Peel off top paper and fit dough into pie plate; remove other paper. Press dough into pie plate and flute edges as you desire. Repeat with second ball of dough. (Makes 2 single-crusts or 1 double-crust.)

To make Filling: In mixing bowl, beat eggs slightly with mixer. Add sugar and salt; mix until dissolved. Add corn syrup and butter; mix well. Stir in pecans. Pour filling into unbaked pie shell. Bake at 350°F for 45-50 minutes or until knife inserted in center of pie comes out clean.

*Norma J. Bobbett, Lutz*

 # Pumpkin Pie

2 eggs
1 (29-ounce) can solid-pack pumpkin
¾ cup sugar
½ teaspoon salt
1 teaspoon cinnamon
½ teaspoon ginger
¼ teaspoon ground cloves
1 (12-ounce) can Carnation evaporated
   milk
1 unbaked pie shell

In large mixing bowl, combine all ingredients in order listed; mix well. Pour filling into unbaked pie shell. Bake at 425°F for 15 minutes, then reduce temperature to 350°F and bake an additional 40-50 minutes or until knife inserted near center of pie comes out clean. Cool.

*Mrs. Lewie A. Hunter, Dunedin*

## Elegant Strawberry Pie

¼ cup sugar
2 tablespoons cornstarch
⅓ cup water
⅓ cup grenadine syrup
1 tablespoon lemon juice
½ cup sliced almonds, toasted
1 (9-inch) pastry shell, baked and
   cooled
1 small package instant vanilla
   pudding mix
1¼ cups milk
1½ cups dairy sour cream
1 pint strawberries, sliced

To make glaze for pie: In saucepan, combine sugar and cornstarch. Blend in water, grenadine syrup, and lemon juice. Cook and stir over medium heat until mixture thickens and bubbles. Cover and cool at room temperature (do not chill).

Sprinkle almonds on bottom of baked pastry shell; set aside. In small bowl, combine pudding mix, milk, and sour cream. Beat at lowest speed of electric mixer for 1 minute. Immediately pour pudding mixture over almonds in pastry shell. Spread one-third of the glaze over pudding mixture. Arrange sliced strawberries on top of glaze in a circular pattern, beginning at outer edge of pie next to crust. Spoon remaining glaze over fruit. Chill for at least 1 hour before serving.

Serves 6-8.

*Florida Department of Agriculture and Consumer Services*

# Strawberry Dream Pie

2 envelopes unflavored gelatin
½ cup half-and-half, chilled
½ cup sugar
Pinch of salt
2 eggs
Few drops of red food coloring
2 tablespoons amaretto
1½ cups fresh strawberries
1 (8-ounce) container whipped topping, thawed (reserve a small amount for top of pie)
1 (10-inch) chocolate pie shell or 1 (9-inch) ready-to-use pie shell (you will have some of the filling left over if you use the packaged shell)
8 chocolate-dipped strawberries (for garnish)

## CHOCOLATE PIE SHELL

1 (10-inch) pie plate
1½ cups ground chocolate cookies
¼ cup (½ stick) butter or margarine, melted

To make Chocolate Pie Shell: Combine ground cookies and butter in pie plate; mix well. Press mixture into bottom and up sides of pie plate. Freeze until needed.

To make Filling: In small bowl, soften gelatin in half-and-half for 10 minutes, then microwave until hot to dissolve gelatin. Pour mixture into blender or food processor container and process on low. Add sugar, salt, eggs, food coloring, and amaretto; blend well. Add strawberries and blend on high to liquefy. Pour into medium-size bowl and chill or freeze until mixture thickens, approximately 30 minutes in the freezer. Stir every 15 minutes. Fold whipped topping into thickened strawberry mixture.

Pile filling into pie shell; pipe reserved whipped topping around edge of pie. Freeze for 1 hour before serving. Garnish with chocolate-dipped strawberries. Cut with wet knife.

Serves 8.

NOTE: This recipe won the Sweepstakes Award at the Florida State Fair and Best of Show at the Pinellas County Fair in 1983.

Shirley J. Myrsiades, Clearwater
Florida Homemaker of the Year, 1982 and 1983

# Strawberry-Rhubarb Pie

## CRUST

*2 cups all-purpose flour*
*½ teaspoon salt*
*½ cup Wesson oil*
*¼ cup cold milk*

## FILLING

*1½ cups frozen or fresh diced rhubarb*
*1½ cups frozen or fresh strawberries*
*4 tablespoons flour*
*¾ cup sugar*
*2 tablespoons butter, melted*
*Sugar (for top crust)*

To make Crust: In mixing bowl, combine flour and salt. Add oil and milk; mix together with a fork. Roll out half of the dough between sheets of waxed paper on a moist board; fit dough into pie plate. Roll out remaining dough for top crust; set aside.

To make Filling: In mixing bowl, combine rhubarb, strawberries, flour, sugar, and butter; mix well.

Pour filling into unbaked pie shell; cover with top crust. Sprinkle top crust with sugar and decorate with dough cut-outs, if desired. Bake at 450°F for 15 minutes, then reduce heat to 350°F and continue baking for approximately 45 minutes.

*Audrey Schroeder, Tampa*

# Sweet Potato Pie

*6 medium sweet potatoes*
*¾ cup (1½ sticks) margarine*
*1½ cups milk*
*1½ teaspoons cinnamon*
*1 teaspoon allspice*
*1½ teaspoons nutmeg*
*3 eggs*
*1 cup brown sugar*
*1 cup white sugar*
*1 teaspoon vanilla extract*
*2 deep-dish frozen pie shells, thawed and unbaked*

Boil sweet potatoes until soft; peel cooked potatoes. In large bowl, combine sweet potatoes, margarine, and milk; mix with hand mixer. Add cinnamon, allspice, and nutmeg. Beat eggs in separate bowl, then add to sweet-potato mixture; blend until smooth. Pour filling into pie crusts. Bake at 350°F for 1 hour 15 minutes.

Serves 12-16.

*Nancy F. Packett, Tallahassee*

# COOKIES

# Mint Stick Brownies
## Best of Show—Young American

½ cup (1 stick) margarine
2 (1-ounce) squares unsweetened
   chocolate
¾ cup sifted flour
½ teaspoon baking powder
¼ teaspoon salt
1 cup sugar
2 eggs
1 teaspoon vanilla
¾ cup miniature chocolate chips

**MINT FROSTING**

⅓ cup margarine, softened
2 cups powdered sugar
1 teaspoon vanilla
⅛ teaspoon peppermint flavoring
3 tablespoons milk
2 drops green food coloring

**CHOCOLATE GLAZE**

1 (1-ounce) square unsweetened
   chocolate
½ teaspoon margarine
½ cup confectioners' sugar
½ tablespoon warm water

Preheat oven to 350°F.

In saucepan, combine margarine and chocolate; heat until melted, then cool. Combine flour, baking powder, and salt; sift together, then set aside. In separate bowl, combine sugar, eggs, and vanilla; slowly mix in chocolate mixture followed by dry ingredients. Stir in chocolate chips. Spoon batter into 8x8x2-inch pan. Bake at 350°F for 30-35 minutes. Cool slightly. Spread Mint Frosting on top of brownie, then drizzle Chocolate Glaze on top of Mint Frosting. Cool, then cut brownies into bars.

To make Mint Frosting: In mixing bowl, combine margarine, powdered sugar, vanilla, peppermint flavoring, milk, and food coloring (use just enough to make a very light green frosting); mix well.

To make Chocolate Glaze: In saucepan, combine chocolate and margarine; heat until melted. Add confectioners' sugar and water; beat well.

Makes 2 dozen brownies.

*Candice Suzanne Shawhan, Sarasota*

# Chocolate Ninja Turtle Cookies

½ cup flour
½ teaspoon baking powder
¼ teaspoon salt
2 tablespoons instant coffee crystals
2 teaspoons vanilla
24 ounces semisweet chocolate chips, divided
4 ounces unsweetened baking chocolate, chopped
¼ cup (½ stick) butter, softened
1½ cups sugar, divided
4 eggs, slightly beaten
2 cups coarsely chopped walnuts
2 cups pecan halves

Preheat oven to 350°F. Line two baking sheets with aluminum foil; set aside.

In medium bowl, combine flour, baking powder, and salt; stir together, then set aside. In small cup, dissolve coffee crystals in vanilla; set aside. In top of double boiler, combine half of the chocolate chips, baking chocolate, and butter; heat over hot water until melted, stirring until smooth. Pour melted chocolate into large mixing bowl; stir in ½ cup sugar, then gradually stir in eggs. Add remaining sugar and coffee mixture; mix well. Blend in dry ingredients. Fold in remaining chocolate chips and walnuts.

Using ¼-cup measure, drop dough two inches apart onto prepared baking sheets. Insert five pecan halves around the bottom edge of each cookie to form four "legs" and a "head." Bake cookies at 350°F for 10-12 minutes or until cookies start to crack. Do not overbake. Cool cookies in pans on wire rack. Store in airtight container for up to five days.

Makes 24 cookies.

*Laura York, Valrico*

 # Chocolate-Dipped Peanut Brittle Fingers

## BUTTER PASTRY

*9 tablespoons (1 stick plus 1
    tablespoon) unsalted butter, softened*
*½ cup plus 1 tablespoon granulated
    sugar*
*1 large egg plus 1 large egg yolk*
*1 teaspoon vanilla extract*
*2¼ cups all-purpose flour*

## PEANUT BRITTLE TOPPING

*¼ cup plus 2 tablespoons light corn
    syrup*
*½ cup light brown sugar, packed*
*4 tablespoons unsalted butter*
*¼ cup heavy whipping cream*
*2 cups coarsely chopped salted roasted
    peanuts*
*1 teaspoon vanilla extract*
*Few drops of lemon juice*

## CHOCOLATE GLAZE

*6 ounces semisweet chocolate, coarsely
    chopped, or 1 cup semisweet or milk-
    chocolate chips*
*2 tablespoons vegetable shortening*

Place a rack in center of oven; preheat oven to 350°F.

To make Butter Pastry: In mixing bowl, combine butter and sugar; beat at medium-high speed of hand-held electric mixer for 2-3 minutes or until mixture is light and fluffy. Stir in egg, egg yolk, and vanilla. Add flour and stir just until combined. Press pastry mixture into ungreased 10½x15½-inch jelly-roll pan (do not use nonstick pan), pressing mixture up sides slightly. Refrigerate dough for 15 minutes. Prick surface of chilled dough with a fork; bake at 350°F for 18-20 minutes or until pastry is lightly browned.

To make Peanut Brittle Topping: In medium saucepan, combine corn syrup and brown sugar; heat over low heat, stirring until sugar is dissolved. Add butter and cream; increase heat to medium-high and bring mixture to rolling boil. Remove pan from heat; stir in peanuts, vanilla, and lemon juice. Pour mixture over baked crust, spreading gently and evenly with a spatula. Bake at 350°F for 15-20 minutes or until topping is bubbly and lightly browned. Remove pan from oven; place on wire rack and cool completely. With a sharp knife, trim off edges, then cut pastry into 1x2-inch bars.

To make Chocolate Glaze: In top of double boiler, combine chocolate and vegetable shortening. Heat over hot, not simmering, water until mixture is melted and smooth, stirring occasionally. Scrape mixture into a shallow bowl. Dip each peanut brittle bar in warm chocolate, coating halfway. Cool bars on wire rack until chocolate is set.

*Laura York, Valrico*

# Double Chocolate Brownies

4 (1-ounce) squares chocolate
1 tablespoon water
2 cups sugar
1 cup (2 sticks) margarine
¼ teaspoon salt
4 eggs
1 cup flour
2 teaspoons vanilla
1 cup chopped walnuts

**TOPPING**

1 cup powdered sugar
4 (1-ounce) squares chocolate, melted
½ cup milk

Combine chocolate and water in saucepan; heat until chocolate is melted, then set aside. In mixing bowl, cream sugar, margarine, and salt; add eggs and beat well. Add flour gradually, then add melted chocolate and vanilla; blend together. Add nuts; mix well. Pour batter into well-greased 9x9-inch pan. Bake at 300°F for 30 minutes. Spread Topping over baked brownies. Return pan to oven for 10 minutes or until Topping is melted. Remove from oven and cut into squares. Serve hot or cold.

To make Topping: In mixing bowl, combine powdered sugar, melted chocolate, and milk; mix thoroughly.

*Helen Postiglione, Tampa*

# Cream Sandwich Cookies

¾ cup brown sugar
1 cup (2 sticks) butter
1 egg yolk
2 cups flour

**FROSTING**

2 tablespoons butter
1½ cups powdered sugar
½ teaspoon vanilla
Milk

Preheat oven to 325°F.

In large bowl, combine brown sugar and butter; beat until light. Add egg yolk; blend well. Add flour; mix well. Form dough into one-inch balls. Place balls on ungreased cookie sheets. Using a fork, flatten balls into 1½-inch cookies. Bake at 325°F for 10-14 minutes. Remove from oven and cool. Spread one teaspoon frosting between two cooled cookies to make a "sandwich." Repeat until all cookies and frosting have been used.

To make Frosting: In saucepan, heat butter until melted; stir in powdered sugar and vanilla. Add enough milk to obtain desired spreading consistency.

Makes 2½ dozen cookies.

*Joyce Downs, Brandon*

## Jewel Cookies
### Best of Show—Youth

4½ cups flour
6 egg yolks, beaten (reserve egg whites)
1 cup sugar
⅓ cup Crisco shortening
1½ cups (3 sticks) margarine, softened
Chopped nuts or coconut
Your favorite jam

In large mixing bowl, combine flour, egg yolks, sugar, shortening, and margarine; mix and knead together. Chill dough for 1 hour. Remove a small amount of dough (it will be hard to handle) and roll out. Cut dough into desired shapes using cookie cutters. Brush half of the cutouts with reserved egg whites, then sprinkle with chopped nuts or coconut. Repeat this process until all of the dough is used, leaving half of the cutouts plain. Place all cutouts on ungreased cookie sheets and bake at 375°F for 10-12 minutes. Remove from oven and cool. Spread plain cookies with your favorite jam, then top with nut- or coconut-topped cookies to make "sandwiches."

NOTE: These cookies freeze very well.

*Julie K. Hunter, Dunedin*

## Magic Cookie Bars

½ cup (1 stick) margarine
1½ cups graham-cracker crumbs
1 (14-ounce) can sweetened condensed milk
1⅓ cups coconut
1 (6-ounce) package chocolate bits (chocolate lovers may use more!)
1 cup chopped nuts

Place margarine in 13x9-inch pan; heat in oven until margarine is melted. Sprinkle graham-cracker crumbs over margarine; mix together and press into pan. Pour sweetened condensed milk evenly over crumbs. Top with coconut, chocolate bits, and nuts; press down firmly. Bake at 350°F (325°F for glass pan) for 25-30 minutes or until lightly browned.

*Ruth Poiles, Dunedin*

## Oatmeal Cookies

1 cup (2 sticks) butter, softened
1 cup granulated sugar
1 cup brown sugar, packed
2 eggs
1 teaspoon vanilla
1½ cups flour
½ teaspoon salt
1 teaspoon baking soda
3 cups rolled oats
2 cups raisins
1¼ cups chopped pecans

In mixing bowl, combine butter and sugars; cream until light and fluffy. Add eggs and vanilla; mix well. Combine flour, salt, and baking soda; add to creamed mixture and mix thoroughly. Stir in rolled oats, raisins, and pecans. Drop batter by level tablespoonfuls onto greased cookie sheet. Bake at 350°F for 13-15 minutes or until golden brown. Cool on cookie sheet for 1 minute, then remove.

*Doris Swank, Naples*

 ## Peanut Butter Cookies

½ cup (1 stick) butter
½ cup chunky peanut butter
½ cup sugar
½ cup brown sugar, packed
1 egg
½ teaspoon vanilla
1¼ cups flour
½ teaspoon baking powder
¾ teaspoon baking soda
¼ teaspoon salt
Granulated sugar

In mixing bowl, combine butter, peanut butter, sugar, brown sugar, egg, and vanilla; cream together. Combine flour, baking powder, baking soda, and salt; add to creamed mixture and mix well. Chill dough for 3 hours. Form level tablespoonfuls of dough into balls; place balls three inches apart on greased cookie sheet. Dip fork in sugar and flatten balls with fork in crisscross pattern. Bake at 350°F for 10-12 minutes or until lightly browned.

*Doris Swank, Naples*

# Macaroons

1½ cups coconut
½ cup sweetened condensed milk
½ teaspoon vanilla

In mixing bowl, combine coconut, sweetened condensed milk, and vanilla; mix well. Drop mixture by teaspoonfuls onto well-greased baking sheets, leaving one inch between cookies. Bake at 350°F for 10-12 minutes or until golden brown. Remove at once from baking sheets.

*Nancy Welker, St. Petersburg Beach*

# Maple Pecan Icebox Cookies

1 cup (2 sticks) butter or margarine
3 cups dark brown sugar
2 eggs, well beaten
2 tablespoons maple flavoring
4 cups cake flour
1 teaspoon soda
1 teaspoon baking powder
½ teaspoon salt
1 cup pecan meats, chopped
3 cups shredded coconut, chopped

In mixing bowl, combine butter and brown sugar; cream together. Add eggs and maple flavoring; mix well. Combine flour, soda, baking powder, and salt; add to creamed mixture and mix thoroughly. Stir in pecans and coconut. Form dough into rolls one inch in diameter; wrap rolls securely in plastic wrap and aluminum foil. Refrigerate rolls for 4-6 hours or overnight. Unwrap rolls, then cut into ¼-inch slices. Bake at 350°F for 7-10 minutes. Cool cookies in pan for 1-2 minutes before removing to cooling rack.

*Julie K. Hunter, Dunedin*

# Snickerdoodles

½ cup (1 stick) butter
½ cup shortening
1½ cups sugar
2 eggs
2¾ cups flour
1 teaspoon baking soda
¼ teaspoon salt
2 teaspoons cream of tartar
2 tablespoons cinnamon
2 tablespoons sugar

In mixing bowl, cream butter, shortening, sugar, and eggs. Combine flour, baking soda, salt, and cream of tartar. Add dry ingredients to creamed mixture; mix well. Combine cinnamon and sugar; set aside. Form dough into one-inch balls. Roll balls in cinnamon-sugar mixture, then place two inches apart on ungreased cookie sheet. Bake at 400°F for 8-10 minutes.

*Doris Swank, Naples*

# Pecan Cookies

1½ cups (3 sticks) butter, softened
1 cup light brown sugar, firmly packed
2 teaspoons granulated sugar
2 teaspoons milk
½ teaspoon baking soda
2½ cups flour (spoon lightly when
    measuring)
2 cups chopped pecans

Preheat oven to 375°F.

In mixing bowl, combine butter and sugars; cream until light and fluffy. Add all remaining ingredients; mix well. Drop batter by rounded teaspoonfuls onto ungreased cookie sheets. Bake at 375°F for 10-12 minutes. Cool for about 1 minute on cookie sheets, then remove to wire racks to cool completely.

Makes about 5 dozen cookies.

*Florida Department of Agriculture and Consumer Services*

 ## Perfect Party Cookies
### Best of Show—Adult

1 cup (2 sticks) butter, softened
⅓ cup whipping cream
2 cups flour
Granulated sugar

**FILLING**

¼ cup (½ stick) butter, softened
¾ cup powdered 10X sugar
1 teaspoon vanilla

**FROSTING**

¼ cup Crisco shortening
3 tablespoons water
1 teaspoon vanilla
Powdered 10X sugar

In mixing bowl, combine butter, whipping cream, and flour; mix thoroughly. Cover and chill. Roll out dough on floured board; cut into desired shapes. Coat both sides of cutouts with sugar, then prick with a fork. Bake at 375°F for 7-9 minutes. Remove from oven and cool. Spread filling over top of one cookie, then top with another cookie to make a "sandwich." Repeat with remaining cookies. Decorate tops of cookie "sandwiches" with frosting.

To make Filling: In mixing bowl, combine butter, powdered sugar, and vanilla; blend together until smooth.

To make Frosting: In mixing bowl, combine shortening, water, vanilla, and enough powdered sugar to obtain desired spreading consistency; blend until smooth.

*Donna Gouhin, Plant City*

# CANDY

## Buckeye Candy
### Best of Show—Young American

3 pounds powdered sugar
2 pounds peanut butter
1 pound butter or margarine, softened
1 bag Nestlé chocolate chips
1/3 bar paraffin wax

In large bowl, combine powdered sugar, peanut butter, and butter; cream together. In top of double boiler, melt chocolate chips over hot water. Add paraffin to melted chocolate and continue to heat until paraffin is melted; mix well. Form creamed mixture into balls, then dip balls in chocolate mixture to coat. Place coated balls on waxed paper until chocolate is set.

*Tina M. Jordan, Crystal River*

## Fancy Butter Pecan Caramels

2 cups sugar
2 cups half-and-half
¾ cup light corn syrup
½ cup (1 stick) butter
½ cup semisweet chocolate chips, melted
64 pecan halves

In heavy saucepan, combine sugar, one cup half-and-half, corn syrup, and butter. Cook over medium heat, stirring occasionally, until mixture comes to a full boil, about 7-8 minutes. Add remaining one cup half-and-half; continue cooking, stirring often, until a small amount of mixture dropped into ice water forms a firm ball or until candy thermometer reaches 245°F, about 35-40 minutes.

Pour mixture into greased 8x8-inch pan. Cover; refrigerate for 1 to 1½ hours to cool. Cut candy into sixty-four pieces. Spoon ½ teaspoon melted chocolate on top of each piece of candy, then press a pecan half into chocolate on each piece. Cover and store in refrigerator.

*Laura York, Valrico*

# Chocolate-Covered Peanut Creams

1 cup peanut butter
1 (7½-ounce) jar marshmallow creme
2 cups sugar
⅔ cup milk
1 teaspoon vanilla
1 pound coating chocolate

In mixing bowl, combine peanut butter and marshmallow creme; mix well. In saucepan, combine sugar and milk; cook until soft-ball stage is reached (236°F). Remove sugar-milk mixture from heat; pour over peanut butter mixture in bowl and beat until smooth. Pour candy into buttered pan; set aside until set, then cut into squares. Melt chocolate. Dip candy squares in chocolate, coating completely. Place coated candies on waxed paper; refrigerate until set.

Makes 30-35 pieces.

NOTE: This recipe was the Purple Rosette Winner (Best of Division) at the Collier County Fair.

*Helen L. Clymer, Marco Island*

 # Cream Mints

4 ounces cream cheese, softened
2½ cups powdered sugar
Mint flavoring
Lemon flavoring
Peppermint flavoring
Food colorings (green, yellow, and red)

In mixing bowl, combine cream cheese and powdered sugar; beat well. Divide mixture into three equal portions. Flavor one portion with mint flavoring, then add green food coloring. Repeat with second portion, adding lemon flavoring and yellow coloring, and with third portion, adding peppermint flavoring and red coloring. Knead each portion separately to blend flavoring and color. Form mixture into small patties, then flatten with a fork. Set aside and let dry overnight.

*Doris Swank, Naples*

# Coconut Bon Bons

40 candy-coating wafers
Coconut dough (available at candy
  supply stores)

Pour water into electric skillet until one-half full. Place deep Corning ware dish in skillet (may need to add more water). Place candy-coating wafers in dish. From the Off position, turn skillet temperature dial just until the light comes on (this is usually high enough to melt candy). Heat until wafers are melted.

Brush melted candy onto a bon-bon form using a small artists' brush. Place form in freezer for 2 minutes to set candy. Form coconut dough into small balls. Press balls into candy shells, filling each within ⅛ inch of top. Continue until all shells are filled. Spoon melted candy onto each bon bon to cover. Return to freezer to set candy, about 2-3 minutes. To remove candies from tray, rap tray gently on a hard surface.

*Doris Swank, Naples*

# Divinity
## (Microwave Recipe)

2¼ cups sugar
½ cup water
½ cup light corn syrup
¼ teaspoon salt
2 egg whites
1½ teaspoons vanilla
½ cup chopped nuts

In two-quart casserole, combine sugar, water, corn syrup, and salt. Loosely cover casserole with a lid or plastic wrap; microwave on high for 5-6 minutes. Uncover and microwave on high for 8-10 minutes or until hard-ball stage is reached (260°F on a microwave-safe candy thermometer). Beat egg whites until stiff. Slowly pour hot syrup over egg whites while beating at high speed of electric mixer. Add vanilla and continue beating for 4-5 minutes or until candy holds its shape. Fold in nuts. Quickly drop mixture by teaspoonfuls onto waxed paper. Cool.

*Nancy Welker, St. Petersburg Beach*

# Wisconsin Cheese Fudge

1 cup (2 sticks) butter, softened
8 ounces pasteurized process cheese,
    cubed
1½ pounds powdered sugar
½ cup cocoa
½ cup nonfat dry milk powder
2 teaspoons vanilla
2 cups coarsely chopped nuts

In saucepan, heat butter and cheese over medium heat until melted; remove from heat. Combine powdered sugar and cocoa; sift together, then add to melted cheese mixture, mixing well. Stir in milk powder, vanilla, and nuts; mix well. Pour mixture into greased 9x9x2-inch pan. Chill until firm, about 1 hour.

Makes 3 pounds candy.

*Sharon Townsend, Gainesville*

# Nut Fudge

3 cups sugar
¾ cup (1½ sticks) butter
6 ounces evaporated milk
1 (12-ounce) package semisweet
    chocolate chips
6 ounces marshmallow creme
1 cup chopped nuts (I use walnuts)
1 teaspoon vanilla

In heavy pot, combine sugar, butter, and evaporated milk. Bring to full, rolling boil, stirring constantly (wear an oven mitt to protect your hand). Reduce heat to medium and continue boiling for 5 minutes, stirring constantly. Remove mixture from heat; add chocolate chips and stir until chips are melted. Add marshmallow creme, nuts, and vanilla; mix well. Pour mixture into 13x9-inch greased baking pan. Allow to cool and it's ready!

*Renee Goodale, Tampa*

## Peanut Brittle
### (Microwave Recipe)
### Best of Show—Adult

1½ cups raw, shelled red-skin peanuts
1 cup sugar
½ cup light corn syrup
⅛ teaspoon salt
1 teaspoon butter
1 teaspoon vanilla
1 teaspoon baking soda

In 1½-quart dish, combine peanuts, sugar, corn syrup, and salt. Microwave on high for 8 minutes, stirring well after 4 minutes. Stir in butter and vanilla, then microwave on high for 2 minutes. Add soda and mix until foamy. Pour mixture onto a greased baking sheet. Cool. Break candy into pieces by picking up pan and dropping it on the counter.

*Marian Conway, Tampa*

## Peanut Brittle

1 cup water
1 cup corn syrup
3½ cups sugar
2½ cups raw peanuts
¼ cup (½ stick) butter
1 tablespoon soda
1 tablespoon vanilla
Pinch of salt

In saucepan, combine water, corn syrup, and sugar. Heat until candy thermometer reaches 250°F, stirring occasionally. Remove from heat; add peanuts and butter. Return to heat and continue cooking until temperature reaches 310°F. Remove from heat; stir in soda, vanilla, and salt. Pour mixture onto a greased marble slab; stretch when cool.

*Sarah Gray, Nokomis*

## Pecan Roll

7 ounces marshmallow creme
1 teaspoon vanilla
¼ teaspoon almond extract
1 pound confectioners' sugar
1 pound caramels
4 cups chopped pecans

Combine marshmallow creme, vanilla, almond extract, and confectioners' sugar, kneading in last of sugar gradually. Divide mixture into eight equal portions, then form each portion into a one-inch roll. Wrap rolls in waxed paper; freeze until quite hard. Melt caramels in top of double boiler. Dip frozen rolls in melted caramel, then roll in chopped pecans. Cool. Store candy in a cool, dry place.

*Alice Hall, Seffner*

## Spiced Nuts

1 cup sugar
½ teaspoon cinnamon
⅓ cup Pet evaporated milk
1½ cups nuts
½ teaspoon vanilla

In saucepan, mix together sugar and cinnamon; stir in evaporated milk. Bring to boil and cook, stirring constantly, until soft-ball stage is reached (236°F). (Mixture will form a soft ball when a small amount is dropped in cold water.) Remove from heat. Add nuts and vanilla; stir until mixture can no longer be stirred. Turn out onto waxed paper, then separate into small pieces. Cool.

Makes 2 cups.

NOTE: Great for gifts.

*Joyce Covington, Brandon*

# BEVERAGES

# Key West Cooler

1½ cups grapefruit juice
1 small ripe banana, cut into chunks
1 kiwi fruit, peeled and sliced
1 tablespoon honey
1 cup ice cubes
Wedges of grapefruit (for garnish)

In blender container, combine grapefruit juice, banana, kiwi, honey, and ice cubes. Cover and blend at high speed until smooth and frothy. Pour into two large, iced daiquiri glasses. Garnish with grapefruit wedges.

Serves 2.

NOTE: Rum or vodka can be added, if desired.

*Florida Department of Citrus*

# Orange Smoothee

1 (6-ounce) can frozen orange juice
   concentrate (undiluted)
1 cup milk
1 cup water
¼ cup sugar
½ teaspoon vanilla
10 ice cubes

Place all ingredients in blender container; cover and process until smooth. Serve immediately.

Serves 6.

*Florida Department of Agriculture and Consumer Services*

# Party Punch

1 cup lemon juice
2 (46-ounce) cans orange juice
2 (46-ounce) cans grapefruit juice
2 (46-ounce) cans pineapple juice
Sugar
Water
1 quart Sprite or 2 bottles champagne

Combine all juices. Make a "simple syrup" by mixing equal parts of sugar and water; sweeten juices with syrup to taste. Just before serving, add Sprite or champagne. Serve over ice.

Serves 50.

*Joyce Covington, Brandon*

## Peachy Florida Nog

1½ cups vanilla ice cream
2 fresh peaches, peeled and pitted, or 1
   (10-ounce) package frozen peach
   slices, thawed
2 eggs

Combine all ingredients in blender container. Cover and blend at medium speed until smooth, about 15 seconds. Serve immediately.

Serves 2-3.

*Florida Department of Agriculture and Consumer Services*

## Purple Monster

2 cups milk
1 cup fresh blueberries
2 tablespoons sugar
1 quart vanilla ice cream
Fresh blueberries (for garnish, if
   desired)

Combine milk, berries, sugar, and one pint (two cups) ice cream in blender container; cover and blend on high speed until smooth. Pour mixture into tall glasses, then top each with a scoop of ice cream. Garnish with fresh blueberries, if desired.

Serves 4-6.

*Florida Department of Agriculture and Consumer Services*

## Russian Tea

2 cups water
4 tea bags
1½ cups sugar
1 teaspoon ground cloves
2 cinnamon sticks
1 (46-ounce) can pineapple juice
2 cups orange juice
1 (12-ounce) can apricot nectar
½ cup lemon juice
2 cups water

Heat water to boiling in saucepan; remove from heat and add tea bags, sugar, cloves, and cinnamon sticks. Set aside to steep for 1 hour. Remove cinnamon sticks. Pour tea into a large pot or electric percolator. Add pineapple juice, orange juice, apricot nectar, lemon juice, and water; stir and heat.

Makes 21 six-ounce servings.

*Florida Department of Agriculture and Consumer Services*

# The T.G.I. Florida

2 cups grapefruit juice
1½ cups tangerine juice
1 cup apricot nectar
1 cup seltzer or club soda
Crushed ice
Slices of red grapefruit, halved (for
    garnish)

Mix together grapefruit and tangerine juices, apricot nectar, and seltzer; pour over crushed ice in tall pitcher. Garnish with grapefruit slices.

Serves 4.

Florida Department of Citrus

# INDEX

For information about our state-fair cookbook publishing program, including ordering information, please contact:

**STATE FAIR BOOKS**
P. O. Box 90314
Indianapolis, IN 46290-0314
Phone - (317) 259-1480 or (317) 251-4517